PSYCHOLOGY OF SUCCESS

ALISON & DAVID PRICE

A PRACTICAL GUIDE

Published in the UK in 2011
by Icon Books Ltd,
Omnibus Business Centre,
39–41 North Road,
London N7 9DP
email: info@iconbooks.co.uk
www.iconbooks.co.uk

Sold in the UK, Europe,
South Africa and Asia
by Faber & Faber Ltd,
Bloomsbury House,
74–77 Great Russell Street,
London WC1B 3DA
or their agents

Distributed in the UK, Europe,
South Africa and Asia
by TBS Ltd,
TBS Distribution Centre,
Colchester Road,
Frating Green,
Colchester CO7 7DW

Published in Australia in 2011
by Allen & Unwin Pty Ltd,
PO Box 8500, 83 Alexander Street,
Crows Nest, NSW 2065

Distributed in Canada
by Penguin Books Canada,
90 Eglinton Avenue East, Suite 700,
Toronto, Ontario M4P 2Y3

Published in the USA in 2011
by Totem Books
Inquiries to: Icon Books Ltd,
Omnibus Business Centre,
39–41 North Road,
London N7 9DP, UK

Distributed to the trade in the USA
by Consortium Book Sales
and Distribution
The Keg House, 34 Thirteenth
Avenue NE, Suite 101,
Minneapolis, MN 55413-1007

ISBN: 978-184831-259-3

Typeset in Avenir by Marie Doherty

Printed and bound in the UK by Clays Ltd, St Ives plc

About the authors

Alison Price is a Chartered Occupational Psychologist and has worked with over 1,500 individuals, inspiring them to make more out of their lives and their careers. She was a semi-finalist in 'Britain's Next Top Coach'.

Alison works with employees and leaders of prestigious organizations, supporting the achievement of peak performance at work. She also lectures on a master's-level course in Business Psychology at a London university.

Alison combines her experience as a keynote speaker, facilitator and Peak Performance Coach with her expertise as a psychologist, to create powerful and lasting results. She offers her services through her company The Success Agents.

David Price has spent over 10 years studying personal effectiveness, models of personal achievement and success. David combines qualifications in Life Coaching, Sports Psychology, Positive Psychology, Peak Performance Coaching and as an NLP Practitioner for integrated effectiveness solutions.

David has applied this knowledge in the commercial industry by mentoring and coaching employees within some of the leading financial services firms.

Authors' note

This book contains frequently-used research and methods. Where we know the source we have been sure to reference it, but our apologies here to the originators of any material if we have overlooked them.

Contents

Introduction

When you meet someone who finally takes action on making their life dreams come true, it is a truly inspiring experience. James was one of those people. He had just turned 40, had a wife and two kids and was a senior manager in a reputable finance company in London.

It was one of those spine-tingling moments when we heard that James had been so inspired by our motivational course that he had made the decision to do something that he had been thinking about for a while. After months of pondering, he had at last committed to emigrating to Australia in search of a better life for himself and his family.

We were absolutely over the moon for James and it was great to see him conquer each of the stages needed to make his dream a reality, one after another. It proved to us the enormous power of motivational coaching in helping people to achieve more in their lives.

However, a few months later we stumbled across a piece of research that stopped us in our tracks. The research was from the fascinating new area of **positive psychology**, a field that looks at the science of optimal wellbeing. It said that, on average, people who emigrate to Australia are only 1–2% happier.

This opened our eyes to a potentially fatal flaw in motivational coaching. It can help you to set a goal and energize you to take action towards it, but what if, after all of the effort you've put into achieving it, it doesn't really have any lasting positive effect? Can that really be called 'success'?

The **psychology of success** is therefore a potent combination of research, theory and evidence from four different disciplines to give you a unique, winning recipe that importantly:

- Helps you to set the **right goals** in the first place
- Guides you to **achieve those goals**, focusing both on the benefits of ultimate achievement, and critically, the process of **enjoying working towards** achieving them
- Uses **sound psychological principles**, with a sprinkle of inspiration, to assist you in bringing your hopes and dreams to fruition.

Sound good so far? We certainly hope so. So, let's take a look at the four disciplines on which the psychology of success is founded.

The first discipline is the traditional field of **psychology**, the scientific study of the mind and resulting behaviour. This field is now well over 100 years old and as such, a wealth of invaluable knowledge has been gained about how humans think, act and change. A particular strength is that the findings of this field are grounded with robust scientific evidence – painstaking research has made sense of what were otherwise anecdotal observations.

However, what is particularly interesting is how history shaped the course of this discipline. After World War II many soldiers came home 'broken' by the horrific experiences of war. So, the American government funded research into how to make miserable people less miserable. As a result, by the year 2000, for every one study in how to optimize the performance of healthy people, there were 21 studies in how to fix broken people. We have therefore learnt a lot about things such as combating depression, or reducing anxiety, but this has historically distracted from research into how to achieve success.

In 1998 psychology took a new direction, with the president of the American Psychological Association, Martin Seligman, highlighting this 21:1 ratio and suggesting that a change of focus was needed. At that moment, **positive psychology** was born, a discipline that, rather than investigating what has gone wrong with human behaviour, seeks to find what has gone right. Positive psychology has been described as the study of human potential, and looks at how to improve normal lives and make people happier, more fulfilled and more productive. This discipline is still in its infancy, and as such the findings are somewhat limited compared to longer-established psychological disciplines. However, an enormous amount has been learned in less than fifteen years and no doubt more critical insights will appear over time.

Of particular benefit is the research into what makes people lastingly fulfilled. Why? Because, if you take the view that success cannot really be considered as such if your achievement makes you miserable, it's important to know what is worth putting your time and effort into achieving before you take any major action. It's very useful to know which basket you should be putting your eggs into.

The third discipline is the field of **motivational coaching**, which has been heavily influenced by individuals such as Anthony Robbins. Motivational coaches have popularized some of the tools and theories from the field of **neuro-linguistic programming (NLP)**. NLP is a system of alternative therapy that focuses on the structure and perception we have of events, so that we can improve our experience of them and better get what we want from them.

It's fair to say that these types of tools and techniques have been questioned for not having the scientific rigour of traditional psychology behind them. However, having used these techniques with over 1,500 people we can confirm that they clearly do have an impact. Also, one of the key issues with motivational coaching as a standalone discipline is that it often focuses on areas such as achieving massive wealth, which society teaches us will make us happy. However science shows that it clearly doesn't. So, the benefit of combining motivational coaching with classic psychology and positive psychology is that you have a more balanced mixture of science coupled with powerful inspiration.

Finally, the psychology of success draws upon the discipline of **sports psychology**. This branch of psychology is dedicated to helping amateur and professional sportsmen and women reach the top of their personal sporting game. While this field is more focused on how athletes can become sporting champions, there are some valuable lessons that can be applied far more widely to help you to achieve a 'gold medal' when working towards your own personal goal.

The four disciplines described above are all well-recognized. You can go to study them on a course and there is common agreement as to what these fields cover. However, there is no such recognized field as the 'psychology of success'. It isn't something that you could go and study at university. However several years ago, after our experience with James emigrating to Australia, we realized that there was a new and exciting niche to be explored, one which combines inspiration from motivational coaching and some of the best research and theory from relevant branches of psychology. So, the psychology of success is a concept that is newly introduced to the world through this book.

This book, *The Psychology of Success*, will look at why you should put effort into achieving success, and will get you fired up to take action. We will then explore what success is for you and will support you as you set out to attain it. Finally, the core of the book will be spent covering powerful techniques to achieve success and make your dreams come true.

Since psychologists love studying memory, and since we want you to be successful in remembering the content of this book, each chapter is structured against a letter of the alphabet to help to prompt your memory. The A–Z is also significant in another way, since in our home country, Great Britain, an A–Z is a map book – something that helps people find their way to their chosen destination.

We hope that our A–Z leads you to find many successes in your life.

Alison & David Price

A: Activation!

*It's only when we truly know and understand that we have
a limited time on Earth – and that we have no way of
knowing when our time is up, we will then begin to live
each day to the fullest, as if it was the only one we had.*

Elisabeth Kübler-Ross

Mike was aged '50-something' when we had the pleasure of meeting him. He was a pleasant and relaxed man, with bright eyes and a smile on his face. Yet despite this, Mike was also quite frankly one of the most *annoying* people that you could meet when running a course on making the most out of your life and potential.

This wasn't because, like some, Mike sat there all day with his arms firmly crossed and a sceptical look on his face that clearly read, 'Go on then, motivate me!' In contrast, he seemed to agree with the ethos of the course and was obviously engaged in learning. Yet despite this, in all the exercises designed to set goals and become energized to take action, Mike was adamant that there was absolutely *nothing* that he wanted to do differently in his life.

A common misconception:

There's no point in changing my life. I'm happy sitting at home in my comfy armchair each evening and watching the television.

Rather than this common misconception, is there a different way to look at life?

The value of hindsight

Time travel may not be possible, but we can seek advice from those older and wiser than us and ask them the question: 'If you could live your life over again, what would you do differently?'

Researcher Richard Leider has dedicated nearly 25 years to interviewing senior citizens, asking them just this question (let's hope that he doesn't regret spending all that time on it!). Fascinatingly, he found that, almost without exception, when senior citizens look back, they say the same things:

- Firstly, make sure that you take regular 'time out' to look at the bigger picture, and to work out what you want from life. You get so caught up in the rat race of life that it usually takes a crisis to make you step back and re-visit what your priorities are.
- Secondly, be more courageous and take more risks. You are most alive when you are learning, growing, stretching and exploring.
- And finally, make sure that you work out, as early as possible in your life, what will make you genuinely fulfilled. Success is often measured in external ways, such as how big your house is or what job title you have, but the internal measure of how happy you feel inside is far more important.

This book will help you to achieve all of these things, so that you don't come to share the same regrets as the senior citizens Richard Leider interviewed. It will inspire you to step back and work out what you want from life, challenging you to ensure that the success that you seek will actually lead to lasting fulfilment. It will then give you the confidence and techniques to help you to achieve your dreams.

A final insight from Richard Leider's research: as you grow older, life picks up speed. As you hit the second half of your life, everything moves faster and all of a sudden you realize that you are in your retirement. Looking back, it is obvious that time is the most precious currency in your life.

1. On a piece of paper, draw a rectangle with 8 squares in it, like the one above.
2. Assume that the boxes represent a person's life expectancy of 80 years. Each box therefore represents 10 years.
3. Shade the number of years that you have already lived (e.g. if you are 40, shade in 4 squares).
4. Now shade off a third of the remainder – this represents the sleeping you are yet to do.

5. Next, shade off 50% of the remainder, as our research derived from the UK's Office of National Statistics Time Use Survey (2005) shows that on average we spend:
    *   5 years of our lives eating and drinking (6.25% of our lives)
    *   8 years doing household chores (10% of our lives)
    *   10 years working and studying (12.5% of our lives)
    *   2 years spent on personal care (2.5% of our lives)
    *   5 years commuting and travelling (6.25% of our lives)
    *   9 years watching television (11.25% of our lives)
    *   1 year spent on meetings (1.25% of our lives)
6. Finally, think of anything else in the daily grind that takes up your time that hasn't already been accounted for above. Shade away.

Consider your reaction to this exercise. How do you feel now? What have you learned about your time and your priorities?

So what will make you change your life?
After several hours of working with Mike, exasperated, we asked him, 'Have you always felt this way? Have you always been confident that there is nothing you want to change in your life?' Mike smiled and said:

No. About four years ago, I was driving on my bike and had an accident and very, very nearly died. Since then I have completely changed my attitude towards life and have made massive changes. I realized how precious it is and that it cannot be taken for granted.

Like Mike, many people are motivated to take action to make the most out of their lives following a wake-up call. Researcher Jonathan Haidt, from the University of Virginia, is fascinated by what happens to people like Mike who suffer a major life trauma.

Haidt learned that many people, far from finding the tremendous struggle makes their lives worse, discover that it helps them to grow. Specifically, it helps people to sort out their priorities in life and causes them to do things that are important to them and that they have perhaps not made time for up to that point. Adversity also acts as a filter – suddenly all of the petty and trivial concerns of everyday life become insignificant.

This message is poignantly highlighted by the story of Simon Weston. Simon was a 21-year-old solider aboard a British ship involved in the Falklands War. On 8 June 1982, enemy forces bombed the ship and Simon was caught in the blast. His body was covered in burns that disfigured him and have required over 70 major operations.

Despite his appalling trauma, in his book, *Moving On*, Simon says:

Getting injured wasn't the worst thing that ever happened to me. In some ways it was even the best. Look at all the positive aspects of my life that have grown from my injuries. In the end, it's not what happens to you that counts, but what you do about it. What matters is where you are going to take your life and how you are going to makes things better.

Since suffering his injuries Simon has become dedicated to helping others, driving him to achieve a number of feats he was otherwise fearful of, including skydiving and running the New York City Marathon.

Seize the day

If many people do take action to make the most out of their lives and potential following a wakeup call, the key message is this: **why wait for a wake-up call to change your life?**

Unless you have the fortune to be a genuine clairvoyant (if indeed such a person exists!) then you will never know what is going to happen to you in life. Although many of us live our lives thinking, 'That's an awful story, but that would never happen to me', the harsh reality of life is that it could.

But more than that, wouldn't it be fantastic if you could reap the benefits of achieving more from your life *without* having to survive a major life trauma. Make this the day that you seize the day.

Imagine that you found out that you only had 24 hours to live.

- What would you do?
- Who would you want to speak to?
- What would you want to say to them?

Now ask yourself: what do I need to do in the next 24 hours!

- Take time out to look at the bigger picture of your life. Extend your comfort zone; take on a little extra risk.
- Your time is very precious; spend it doing what will be most rewarding.

 Get activated now, or in other words:

> *Dig a well before you are thirsty.*
> Harvey Mackay

B: Begin with the end in mind

*The trouble with the rat race is that even if you win,
you're still a rat.*

Lily Tomlin

Did you know that a study of the richest Americans revealed that 37% are less happy than the average American? If these people had been pursuing wealth as a means of happiness, that's what we would call being '**successfully unsuccessful**'.

So, before we give you powerful techniques that will rocket power you to achieve your goal of becoming a multi-millionaire, we want to make sure that you are aiming for the right thing.

Drawing upon Stephen Covey's 'jungle clearing' story as an analogy: it doesn't matter how successful you are at felling trees and clearing undergrowth, or indeed how hard you work, if ultimately you are in the *wrong jungle*.

 Before we explore any further, find a blank piece of paper and draw a picture to represent your dream life. Ask yourself, if I could make my life as good as it possibly could be, what would it look like?

It is important to remember this is about what makes *you* happy, not other people. What would your 10/10 life be?

If you don't want to draw your ideal life, have a go thinking about your dream life using our FLOURISH model:

F: Friends – the people who you socialize with
L: Love – your romantic relationships
O: Occupation – how you spend your 'working' time
U: Usual environment – your home, its setting and the lifestyle opportunities it offers
R: Relatives – your relationships with your family members
I: Income – your personal finances
S: Spare time – how you spend your 'free' time
H: Health – your physical wellbeing

How would you FLOURISH?

Why do people end up being 'successfully unsuccessful?'

Although it has been challenged as being somewhat over-simplistic, Abraham Maslow's famous **hierarchy of needs** can still be really helpful in understanding why people end up in 'the wrong jungle' in the first place.

First here's a quick overview of what the hierarchy of needs is: in 1943, Maslow proposed that we have five different types of needs. They all need to be satisfied, but critically, in the following order:

1. **Basic needs** – things we can't survive without, such as air, water, food and shelter, then;
2. **Safety needs** – like protection from physical harm or having the financial security to continue to support our basic needs, then;
3. **Social needs** – satisfying our human requirement for companionship and involvement with others, then;
4. **Esteem needs** – the requirement to be respected and valued or to be able to display signs of wealth and prestige, and finally;
5. **Self-actualization** – the need to be everything that you are capable of being, and reaching your full potential in life.

The hierarchy of needs in action

CASE STUDY To see how the hierarchy of needs plays out in everyday life, let's follow the story of Joe Average, who has recently graduated from university.

Over the past three years Joe has spent way too much money on beer and he is now officially broke, so he heads straight back to Mum and Dad to put a roof over his head and food on the table, therefore satisfying his **basic needs** (and clearly to satisfy the basic need of having his washing done for him too!).

After weeks of him loafing around the house watching daytime television, Joe's mother gives him a kick up the backside and sends him down to the local temp agency to get a job. Joe somehow manages to land himself a low-level job in a good company. He begins to get a regular income and is able to pay for his own food, contribute some rent and begin to pay off his debts, therefore meeting some **safety needs**.

Joe has also made some new friends at work and has even found a girlfriend (that his mother actually likes), ticking lots of boxes in terms of his **social needs**. Joe then manages to get a permanent job in his company. The job is still nowhere near his dream job, but the pay is much better, and over the years he manages to do quite well at it. He gets promoted, becomes more qualified and earns the words 'manager' and then 'senior manager' in his job title. Joe's **esteem needs** are comfortably met, especially with his nice new BMW convertible decorating the car park every day. He even manages to marry the girl that his mother liked.

But Joe hits 40 and his world is rocked by the sudden and unexpected death of his mother. He is haunted by his last phone call to her, when he had to cancel coming round to see her for dinner because he was asked to prepare a work presentation at short notice. Joe realizes that although he has a nice wife, he actually spends very little time with her and instead passes a lot of his existence (he can't call it 'life') sitting in his glass box of an office doing a job he doesn't enjoy and never even wanted in the first place. There's no time for the gym and so now not only is he the proud owner of a set of BMW tyres, but also a hefty 'spare tyre' around his waist.

Then, to top it all off, he receives notice that he has been made redundant. A harsh moment of reality strikes – Joe should have prioritized dinner with his mother over the now pointless meeting. At the time, she didn't seem important enough.

The point of this story is that many of us drift through life, very successfully climbing the hierarchy of needs, reaching close (but not close enough) to the top. This is being successfully unsuccessful.

> *If you don't know where you are going, you'll probably end up someplace else.*
> Lawrence J. Peter

Reaching real success

The problem is that we can reach a point of realization where we find that, because we didn't 'begin with the end in mind', we are near the top of the hierarchy, but our current life cannot support us to move any higher. We are stuck. It often takes a life crisis, like bereavement or a redundancy, to get us to stop and think what we ultimately want from our lives.

But there is an even more sobering question to consider when trying to begin with the end in mind. That is: 'Do

I actually have the *right* end in mind?' We have asked you to draw what 10/10 life would look like for you, and that was asking you to begin with the end in mind. Now we want to make the crucial point that even if you made that piece of paper come true, you *still* might not be happy.

THINK ABOUT IT

Imagine that you have just picked up the keys to your very own, multi-million dollar house in glamorous Hollywood. It's stunning – marble floors, contemporary but elegant bathrooms with the highest specification of fixtures and fittings. You have your very own swimming pool and hot tub. Life is perfect.

As you pull up to the impressive gates of your new home for the first time as the owner, you glance up the hill next to you and see Jennifer Aniston's hill top mansion. With a pang of envy you think, 'What would it be like to live in a house with that view?'

A critical piece of advice from this chapter: when considering what your dream life would be like, be aware of the research that shows us that even when you are really successful, you quickly adapt to what you acquire and you simply want more.

This is what psychologists call the principle of **hedonic adaptation**. For example, when you first climb into your brand new car, you feel a buzz of excitement. When you climb in the second time, it's exciting, but less so. By the 547th time you get into the same car it barely has any impact on you at all.

This may help to explain why the richest Americans aren't happier than the average American – they've adapted to their wealth and still have yet to reach the top of the hierarchy of needs or discover what will really make them happy. The impact of wealth on personal happiness is well summed up by the late David Lykken, who was Professor of Psychology and Psychiatry at the University of Minnesota: 'People who go to work in their overalls on the bus are just as happy, on average, as those in suits who drive to work in their own Mercedes.'

Achieving genuine success

Many people define success in terms of money or possessions. However, an increasing amount of research makes it clear that most people don't understand the difference between what they *think* will make them happy and what will *actually* make them happy.

I'm sure we aren't the only people to look out of the window on a miserable cold, wet British day and think how much happier we would be if we lived in a sunnier climate. We are therefore fascinated by a piece of research in Martin Seligman's book, *Authentic Happiness*. This research found that people from Nebraska (who live through harsh winter weather) *think* that they would be happier if they lived in California, but intriguingly there is *no* difference in happiness levels between people in Nebraska and California. We perhaps forget that many of the things that stress us out would still stress us out even if we lived in a perfect climate, and perhaps don't appreciate how quickly we take our surroundings for granted.

So then, when beginning with the end in mind, what should we focus on if we want to achieve real success and fulfilment in our lives? The next chapter will show you a crucial key to cracking the secret of fulfilment. However, in the meantime here are a couple of other things that are worth doing.

Firstly, it's worth setting goals aimed at making your relationships as strong as they can be. Research shows that having focused, trusting social relationships makes us happy.

Secondly, wherever possible, set goals that include doing something that is meaningful to you. It can be difficult to comprehend what your purpose is in life, but it's certainly worth trying to work out sooner rather than later what this is and aligning yourself with it. The clear message from modern research and the wise words of our elders is that living life with a sense of purpose and meaning is ultimately what makes you feel fulfilled.

One way you could begin to discover what it is that would fulfil you is to answer this question we regularly pose: 'If money was no object, what would you want to spend your time doing?'

Look back at the list of life goals that you made in the previous exercise. In the light of what you have just read about hedonic adaptation, the need for wealth and what really brings fulfilment in life ask yourself, 'Am I focusing my precious time and energy in the right place?'

People can find that one of the most liberating moments of their life is when they realize that they don't need to constantly strive to move to a bigger house, get a bigger car or get a better office. They are liberated because they are able to revisit their priorities and are no longer caught up in the never-ending spiral of constantly wanting more. You may have heard of a phenomenon called 'yacht envy' which occurs frequently in Monaco when multi-millionaires moor their luxury boat next to an even better one and feel that they need an upgrade. If that sounds ridiculous to you, remember that we probably all fall into a similar trap.

- Make sure you're pursuing success in the 'right jungle'.
- Be aware of your own hierarchy of needs and how all aspects of your life are contributing to or detracting from these.

- Identify what self-actualization – the fulfilment of your potential – really means for you.

IF YOU REMEMBER ONE THING This book rocket powers you to achieve success, but before we do that we want to be sure that all of your hard effort will pay off and make you happy (which in our opinion is real success). It is always important to begin with the end in mind and remember that having lots of money doesn't mean that you have reached the top of the hierarchy.

C: Current versus future

Too often we are so preoccupied with the destination,
we forget the journey.

Unknown

In the last chapter we promised you a secret key to help you to crack the challenge of finding lasting fulfilment in life. That secret key is all to do with burgers – well, what else would it be! There are four types of burger in life. Let's look at them in turn …

The 'outside a nightclub' burger

You've had a great night out, it's 2 a.m. and you stumble out of the nightclub with your rather merry friends. Then you get the munchies. And like a ray of light shining down in the car park, you see a van and tantalizing burger smells are wafting from it. You dig out what change you have left and purchase a burger, drooling at the mouth. You sink your teeth into it like a vampire. And then suddenly, you sober up and realize:

The burger tastes awful (CURRENT) and it's really unhealthy for you (FUTURE).

The 'health farm' burger

You're at a health farm that is lovely except for one thing. All your favourite foods – French fries, chocolate, biscuits, cake, doughnuts – are well and truly banned. But like a glimmer of hope on the menu, amongst the rye bread and lentil soup, you spot a burger. You await your order with glee, until it turns up and you realize that it's a pile of nasty, mashed-up beans with so much greenery it resembles a forest.

The burger tastes awful (CURRENT) but at least it's healthy for you (FUTURE).

The 'fast food' burger

Have you ever had the craving for a fast food burger? Maybe it doesn't happen very often, but when the thought strikes, you cannot rest until you have one … and we confess, it always turns into two hamburgers, large fries and a milkshake!

The burger tastes yummy (CURRENT) but it's really unhealthy for you (FUTURE).

The 'homemade' burger

It's a beautiful summer's day and you are having a barbecue with your friends in your garden. While you're enjoying the sun (wearing plenty of high factor sun cream), you have the pleasure of tucking into a tasty homemade burger, made of lean organic beef, with no preservatives, housed in a delicious granary bun with some fresh and crispy salad.

The burger tastes yummy (CURRENT) and it's healthy for you (FUTURE).

Imagine that the burger is an analogy for the way that people live their lives. The four types of burgers represent four types of people:

'Outside a nightclub' burger: people who are miserable now and aren't working towards anything positive in the future.

'Health farm' burger: people who are miserable now but it will be worth it, because they are working hard towards success in the future.

'Fast food' burger: people who live for the moment and don't mind that they aren't building a firm foundation for a positive future.

'Homemade' burger: people who both enjoy their lives now and, through what they are doing, are building an exciting future.

Try to think of a person you know who represents each type of burger. Which type of burger are you most like?

Failing to enjoy the journey

Psychologist Tal Ben-Shahar is the creator of the burger model (from which these analogies are inspired) and his teachings are extremely insightful. He explains that success is not a moment in time when you 'arrive and are happy'. True success is about **enjoying the journey towards a**

destination that you deem to be valuable. It's all about being a homemade burger.

Tal Ben-Shahar became one of Harvard's most popular lecturers. However, being a Harvard guru was not always his chosen career path and indeed his life story (including months of abstinence from eating junk food and craving burgers) has been highly influential in his teachings.

Between the tender ages of 11 and 16, Ben-Shahar was involved in what he describes as a mental and physical battle with himself. His dream: to become the Israeli national squash champion. He had lived by the principle 'no pain, no gain', working tirelessly towards the moment that he would officially be 'successful' and reap the feelings of ecstasy associated with achieving this outstanding victory. And, at the age of just 16, his lofty ambition was realized. Ben-Shahar describes feelings of elation as he celebrated that night with his friends and family.

Now ask yourself this question: if you have had to put your life on hold for five years, gruellingly working towards this immensely challenging goal, once you achieved it, how long would the elation last in return? Five years? One year? Six months?

For Ben-Shahar, this feeling did not even last for 24 hours. On the very night of his victory, he felt crushed, not elated. This realization would change the course of his life forever, as well as the lives of many who read his books or listen to his fascinating lectures. Tal Ben-Shahar isn't the only person to have felt like this.

Can you imagine what it must have been like to be the first person ever to reach the top of Mount Everest? What would you have thought? How would you have felt?

Well, you may be surprised to hear that in an interview with Forbes, Sir Edmund Hilary himself recounts the fact that while standing on the top of the world, he instinctively glanced over to an unclimbed neighbouring peak, Mount Makalu, and began working out how to climb it. At the very moment of success, he was already looking for the next challenge.

Stepping into the rat-race

Many people are caught up in the rat race of life. They are prepared to trade their emotional wellbeing in the present for the opportunity to achieve so-called 'success'. They are constantly eating 'health farm' burgers, never allowing themselves to enjoy the here and now. And perhaps most worrying of all, this rat-race existence is exactly what we are taught by those who want the very best from us – our parents and teachers.

Think back to when you were a child. Were you told, 'If you study hard, then you'll get good grades.'? Then when you got the good grades, were you told, 'Keep studying away, if you do, you'll get a good degree.'? Then when you graduated what were you told? 'Just work hard for a few years to get a decent start in your career.'? If you did then the message became, 'If you put long hours in then you'll get promoted and be really successful.' As you grow a little older, have you been told, 'Keep working, it's worth it because you will build up a good pension and then you will be able to enjoy your retirement.'?

We met a young lady called Hannah with whom this really resonated. She was in her mid-twenties and said that her parents lived by these values and had passed them on to her. They had previously seemed to make a lot of sense. Then, one day, as her father was working hard and just six weeks away from his well earned retirement, he died suddenly and without warning.

Choosing the right burger

Goals can be a great way to find more success and fulfilment in your life. But what is absolutely critical is that you pick goals where you get genuine pleasure from working towards them, as well as from achieving them.

Clearly there's no point in aiming to be an 'outside a nightclub' burger – after all, who wants to be miserable and create a bad future for themselves?

But, having learned about Hannah's dad dying six weeks before his retirement, you might well ask yourself: 'Should I just live for the moment? Maybe I should just forget about my career or saving for the future and go to travel the world and experience things and – to hell with being sensible!'

If you are thinking this, perhaps challenge yourself and think, 'If I ate a junk food burger for three meals a day for the next year, how would I feel at the end of it?' As we discussed in the previous chapter, the principle of hedonic adaptation may kick in and something that was pleasurable could quickly lose its appeal. Also, think of the impact on your long-term health. By living for the moment, are you limiting your potential for good results in the future?

We are advocating having your cake and eating it. You probably will enjoy your barbecued burger in the sun just as much (if not more) than a batch-cooked greasy burger wrapped in greaseproof paper (suddenly it doesn't seem so appealing does it?). And at the same time, you can be working towards a future that you really want and that will bring you the success and happiness that you deserve.

 Think about a particular destination that you would like to arrive at in the future. In other words, a goal that would make you very happy upon achieving it.

Now, on a scale of 1–10, rate how much you think that you could enjoy working towards that goal (1 being not at all, 10 being totally).

Reflect: what have I learnt from this?

Your aim: be confident that you have set yourself the right goal – something that you will both enjoy achieving AND working towards.

- Ensure what you are aiming for in life will be fulfilling.
- Ensure that the journey you will take to achieve these aims is one you will enjoy.
- Make sure, if you're living a burger that doesn't taste good, or that isn't good for you in the future, that you find a way to order a better one.

Lasting, fulfilling success requires that you balance enjoyment at the current time with payoffs in the future. Wherever you can, choose a path that leads to you enjoying both the journey and the destination.

Related areas to this topic

Some people find it hard to work out what they should aim for in life. If this is still the case for you, we recommend that you take time out to read more books on this topic, such as *Happier* by Tal Ben-Shahar, *The Power of Purpose* by Richard Leider and *Authentic Happiness* by Martin Seligman. These books will help you to gain an insight into where it's valuable to focus your precious energy.

The beginning of this book has concentrated on why it's important to proactively seek to make the most out of your life. It has given you techniques to help you to verify that you have set yourself the right goals. It's crucial that your goals are actually worth the effort needed to achieve them. As we said previously, there is no point in successfully achieving the wrong goals in life.

If you are confident that you know where you are headed, now is the time to get fired up. You are about to embark upon the exciting journey of achieving success.

D: Dare to dream

If we did all of the things that we are capable of doing,
we would literally astound ourselves.

Thomas Edison

Our good friend Zahra, who is now a teacher, was very much inspired by her own French teacher, Mrs Neville. On the first day of Zahra's two-year GCSE course, Mrs Neville made a bold statement to her new class, 'With some hard work, every person in this class will get a grade A or A* in their French GCSE exam.' As you might expect with teenagers the response was, 'Yeah right Miss, whatever!' In fact, Zahra thought that Mrs Neville was completely deluded (although to be fair, that was her opinion of most teachers ... and now she is one – oh the irony).

Mrs Neville ignored this lack of belief. For two years she kept telling the class that indeed every single pupil *would* get an A or an A*. In fact, she said it so often that after a while the students came to realize that their teacher, deluded or not, genuinely, 100% believed that the whole class would actually achieve these grades. Gradually, Mrs Neville's beliefs began to rub off on the students.

And on results day, what do you think happened? Every single pupil in the class did get a grade A or A*! No other class in the entire set of GCSE results had a success rate of 100% of students achieving these top grades. This included the other French class, which comprised students of a similar calibre to Mrs Neville's class, taught by a different teacher but using exactly the same syllabus and textbooks.

So the raw ability of the children in Mrs Neville's class was no different to the raw ability of other classes. There was no particular reason why Mrs Neville's class should totally outstrip the others.

So why do you think that this occurred?

Mrs Neville's success could well be explained by a very powerful technique. She had created a positive **self-fulfilling prophecy**.

Sociologist Robert Merton is credited with coining the term 'self-fulfilling prophecy' in 1968. A self-fulfilling prophecy is, in the beginning, a *false* definition of the situation, but one which evokes new behaviour that makes that originally false conception come true.

The secret behind a self-fulfilling prophecy is that your positive (or negative) belief about a situation makes you take on a different attitude and display different behaviour to someone who has not got that same belief.

For example, Zahra commented that her French class 'worked their socks off', because their teacher made it a challenge for all of the class to get top grades and, importantly, because she had instilled a belief in them that putting in the extra effort was worth it, as they would all reap the benefits of top grades. In contrast, the other class didn't have so much expectation of success, didn't focus as much on achieving their potential and probably didn't try as hard as a result.

THINK ABOUT IT

Have you ever experienced a self-fulfilling prophecy? Or can you recall a time when you have heard of, read about or seen an example of one?

The power of beliefs

So having positive belief in our capability, even if they're not strictly justified (not just yet anyway), can help us to achieve far better results than someone who has a negative or non-beneficial belief about their capability and doesn't even try. Perhaps now you can begin to see the enormous power of daring to dream.

This all sounds great in theory but people often challenge us with this:

I see what you're saying, but if you really don't believe you can do something, it's very hard to make yourself think that you can.

This is certainly a valid comment and the sad fact of the matter is that we aren't all lucky enough to have a Mrs Neville to help us believe in ourselves. Sometimes you have to do this for yourself. But the million-dollar question that follows then is:

How do you believe that you can do something that you don't believe that you can do?

34

TRY IT NOW! Have you ever achieved something that, at some point prior to achieving it, you really didn't think that you could? Think of as many examples as you can.

Think about the lessons you can draw from achieving these things, such as:

- I almost gave up but I had a last shot and succeeded, so I was almost there already.
- I knew exactly what I wanted and just kept trying until I achieved it.
- I'm glad that I aimed high and didn't settle for second best.

Tapping into your potential

Something that's vital to achieving more success in your life is the opening up of your mind to the fact that you *can* do things that you might think are absolutely impossible. A belief is not a fact. You can do so much more than you think you can.

Once you understand that you *are* capable of doing things that you really don't believe that you can do, the world becomes your oyster. You can start attempting things in your life that you absolutely dream of, but which you were convinced were outside your capability. The more you realize that you can do things you don't believe that you can, the more this becomes a self-fulfilling prophecy.

When you know you can't do something, you don't even try – and then it is an absolute certainty that you will not succeed. Contrast this to people who realize that their dreams are possible – they just haven't achieved them yet. These people take action, and with sustained effort and motivation they will succeed in achieving their goals.

 Have a go at the 25-goal challenge! You have five minutes to list down 25 goals. They can be anything you like, for example:

- Places you would like to visit
- Things you would like to own
- Experiences that you would like to have.

Just remember, be specific and don't be afraid to set your sights high (one lady put 'go to the moon/feel weightlessness' on her list).

Okay, you have five minutes to list down your 25 goals. Go for it!

The results of the 25-goal challenge can be really impressive. For example, Louise, the first person we know who tried this exercise, had already achieved fourteen out of her 25 goals within eighteen months. These included 'finding a man', and she is now married. Interestingly, of the fourteen goals that she achieved, eight of them were the first (and most important) ones that she listed, so hopefully you will also achieve the important goals at the top of your list.

One of Louise's goals was to see a blue whale. Like anyone who has ever been to the world-famous Natural History Museum in London, Louise had been inspired by the enormity of the blue whale since the age of 7, when she went on a school trip and saw the museum's gigantic model of one. Of course blue whales are so rare and so notoriously difficult to see that she never thought it would be possible. She had spent twenty years wanting to see a blue whale but had never done anything about it.

But because she had put the goal on paper, just a few weeks later Louise booked a fourteen-day eco-holiday to the Azores to help do research on whales. As luck would have it, in the last hour of the last day of her trip, imagine what floated by and did an elegant dive down towards the ocean floor, showing the full beauty of its enormous, graceful tail. Such a sighting is by no means guaranteed but you simply have to believe that the impossible is, in fact, possible and have a go. You never know what might happen.

But what about those people on the X-Factor ...

You may well be sitting reading this chapter and thinking about all of those people who blindly audition for the X-Factor – the ones who are tone deaf and leave feeling unhappy and disappointed because they didn't get selected to go through to the next round. When running training courses, this is a very common (and fair) challenge that our audience makes. Our take on this comes down to how much you want something. If you truly, utterly and completely want to be a singer you need to be dedicated to achieving it (which requires far more than just turning up at an X-Factor audition). There is a lot of truth in the saying that 'practice makes perfect'. Even talented people some-times need more practice – look at Alexandra Burke who came close but not close enough to the final rounds of the British X-Factor competition in 2005 and then after much effort went on to win the competition in 2008.

In a situation where you want to win the metaphorical X-Factor but you have zero talent, it is also well worth ask-ing yourself, 'Why do I want to achieve this? What would this success bring to me?' Is it that you actually want to be a singer or simply that you want the trappings of suc-cess which come with being a pop-star? If it's the latter, it might be worth asking yourself, 'Is there another way that I can achieve the same outcomes which I am more naturally suited to and enjoy?' After all, 'There's more than one way to skin a cat.'

Next time you are at your local supermarket, pick up a photo album that holds 50 photos and a pack of at least 25 postcards. On each postcard, write one of your 25 goals. When you have achieved your goal, take a photo of you achieving it and place it in the album with the date that you achieved it on. Begin collecting a book of magical memories.

- Dare to dream! We don't have to yet be capable of achieving our goal, we just have to believe that we can and act accordingly.
- You can do more than you think possible, you just need to believe that you can and work towards it.

 Whether you have everything you need to succeed, or whether you're not there just yet, believe first and foremost that you can succeed.

If you think that you can or you think that you can't,
you're right.

Henry Ford

E: Effort

When I played with Michael Jordan on the Olympics team, there was a huge gap between his ability and the ability of the other great players on that team. But what impressed me was that he was always the first one on the floor and the last one to leave.

Steve Alford, NBA player and Olympic gold medallist

What does it take to become the greatest Olympic athlete of all time? Aged just 23, Michael Phelps became very well qualified to answer that question after becoming the first person ever to win eight gold medals at a single Olympic Games. And to top it all off, he has been reported to have earned between $12 and 15 million as a result of his achievement, through sponsorship and speaking engagements. In his own words, 'That's pretty good for a swimmer.'

But this success wasn't just the result of luck or good fortune. An absolutely critical aspect underpinning his achievements was the dedicated, sustained effort he channelled towards his goal. For over twelve years, Phelps trained virtually non-stop and his life was dominated by thousands of hours spent staring at the bottom of a pool. This was by no means always fun. His coach made him do what Phelps describes as 'horrible, horrible work-outs', such as swimming 10,000 meters as fast as he could (which takes about two and a half hours – ouch!).

In an interview with America's CBS news, Phelps's coach Bob Bowman revealed that for about 5 years Phelps did not take a single day off, not even Christmas Day. Training on his birthday was a given – he trained twice on his birthday!

What makes the difference between good and outstanding?

A fascinating piece of research, conducted by psychologist Anders Ericsson, can help answer this question. With the help of the tutors, students at Berlin's elite Academy of Music were classified into three groups. The first group were students that it was judged would never be good enough to play professionally and who were destined to have careers as music teachers. The second group were considered to be good, those who would make it as professional musicians. The third group were the stars, those the tutors thought had the potential to be world-class musicians.

Staggeringly, a single key factor correlated with how good the students were. Perhaps surprisingly, this was nothing more than the number of hours of practice that they had done over their lifetime.

On average, those students in the lowest calibre group totalled 4,000 hours of practice; students in the 'good' group totalled an average of approximately 8,000 hours whereas students in the top group had each practiced for approximately 10,000 hours. The fascinating thing was that Ericsson could not find any 'natural' talents – people in the top group who had not put in the hours. Practice was the key to everyone's success.

This research shows that people do not pick up a violin and become instant geniuses – far from it. Instead 2,000 extra hours of practice (that's the equivalent of 250 extra solid, eight-hour working days) was the difference between being good and outstanding.

THINK ABOUT IT

To achieve their goals of outstanding professional success, both the musicians and Michael Phelps had to put in hours and hours of practice. Think of the thing that you would like to achieve most from your 25-goal list challenge. What effort do you need to put in to achieve your goal? Think of as many things that you need to do as possible.

Big goals need big efforts because they give big rewards

When asked what motivated him to train every day for five years, Phelps replied:

It was wanting to do something that no-one had ever done before. That's what got me out of bed every day.

This is an example of what psychologists call the **effort heuristic**. The effort heuristic (heuristic generally means 'rule of thumb') is the amount of effort a person will put into trying to achieve something, as determined by the value they place on that goal. If the goal is of little importance to them, the amount of effort a person is willing to put into reaching it is going to be lower. So, the effort we put in equals the reward that we expect to get as a result of our effort.

Through our experience of working with a wide range of people and supporting them to achieve their goals, we have consistently found one thing to determine whether or not they are ultimately successful: *how much they want to achieve their goal*. In other words, the more they want their goal, the more effort they are prepared to put in and the more successful they are likely to be.

We cannot emphasize enough that, if you want to achieve something really difficult, in order to be able to keep putting in sustained effort and to succeed, you have to *really want* to achieve your goal.

How do you keep motivated to put in the effort?

When you find that you would like to achieve your goal but you are struggling to stay motivated and put the effort in, remember what the effort heuristic teaches us – the amount of effort that you put in will be equal to how much you want to achieve your goal.

So, if your goal just feels like too much hard work and you are getting despondent, ask yourself whether there is any way that you can reduce the amount of **perceived**

effort that you need to put in, by changing how you try to achieve the goal, so that you enjoy the process of working towards it more.

What stops you from achieving your goals?

 Think about the goal that you have set yourself. What is the single most important thing that holds you back from achieving it?

We have asked this question of hundreds of people. One of the most common answers is, 'I don't have enough time', for example:

- 'I'd like to get fitter, but I work too many long hours to go to the gym.'
- 'It would be nice to have more contact with my parents, but there aren't enough hours in the day when you have kids.'
- 'I want to find a partner, but I'm always at work.'

So just how do we spend our time?

Guess what the third most common use of our time is after sleeping and working or studying? The answer is watching television! On average women spend 2 hours 30 minutes a day watching television/DVDs or listening to music for leisure. But the worst offenders are men, for whom it's almost 3 hours. This is more than enough time to go to the gym, speak to your mother or put a profile on an internet dating site and go out for a drink with a friend you haven't yet met.

So when there probably is some spare time in our day, why don't we utilize it? Sometimes fear can hold us back (many people might be daunted by the prospect of internet dating, but hopefully you aren't scared of talking to your mother!). If you are struggling to achieve your goal and a lack of time is the genuine answer, it's also worth asking yourself, 'How important is this to me?'

If it *is* important to you it *is* worth finding the time. Here's why ...

Think about the goal that you would like to achieve. Picture this:

- You've read this book today, but you've no time to take action on your goal. You can't quite be bothered, so you do nothing.
- By the end of the week you still haven't taken any action. Lots of things just got in the way. How do you feel about your goal?
- It's now been over a month. Picture yourself still having made no progress. What does this say about you? What are you saying to yourself? What are other people thinking about you?

45

- A year later it's the same story. How do you feel about yourself and what you have been able to achieve?
- Three years later, you've got nowhere. See yourself in the future. Nothing has changed, things are exactly the same.

Now, rewind:

- It's the present day and although you are busy, you made a decision to take a step, big or small towards achieving your goal. What is that step? How do you feel when you've done it?
- With momentum on your side, you feel energized for the rest of the week, and you take further action and make more progress. How are you feeling about your goal?
- By the end of the month, you are really starting to reap the benefits of your hard work. What does this say about you? What are you saying to yourself? What are other people thinking about you?
- A year later, things are so different to how they were. Think about what you have been able to achieve. How do you feel about yourself?
- See yourself three years in the future and the successes you've achieved in that time. Picture how great you feel.

Ask yourself: what is the step you need to take *right now*?

- If your goal is going to be worth it you will have to put the effort into achieving it.
- The more you want to achieve the goal and the more you can enjoy the achieving of it, the better motivated you will be to put the effort into it.
- Identify the events in your life that are stealing your time and ask yourself, 'Is there something more important I could be using this time for?' And then go and do what is more important.

What separates a talented individual from a successful one is a lot of hard work.

Stephen King

F: Fear

*Nothing has meaning except for the meaning we give
to it ourselves.*

T. Harv Eker

In our household we are totally divided when it comes to our opinion on spiders lurking on the ceiling. David sits in the 'it's just a spider' camp and Alison sits in the 'it's a completely hideous tarantula' camp.

So when we ask the question, 'Is the spider scary?' who's answer is right? Clearly, Alison thinks it's her – she thinks the wife is *always* right by default!

In all seriousness, we are both right. The spider *is* scary to one person but *not* the other. As it says at the start of this chapter, nothing has meaning except for the meaning that we give to it ourselves.

What is most significant is the contrasting impact that the spider has upon our respective behaviours. When David spots one of those large, common house spiders, he just gets on with what he is doing. When Alison spots a spider, she screams and runs a mile.

Our **perceptions** affect our **behaviour**, even though our **perceptions** are not necessarily real. The **outcome** of the resulting **behaviour** can be positive or negative. If you don't like the **outcome** that you are getting based on that **perception**, then you need to ask yourself, 'Is what I believe actually real?'

So, if you are scared of taking action towards making your goal happen, and if it's affecting your behaviour and holding you back, it's time to ask, 'Just how real is this fear anyway?'

 Overcoming fears can be a vital and necessary step for people in achieving their goals. Therefore this chapter will look at how you can learn to do this.

In preparation for working on this topic, brainstorm any fears that you have related to achieving your goal down the left-hand side of a page. On the right-hand side, list the impact that this fear is having on your behaviour. Here is an example of how this could look:

Fear about my goal	Impact on my behaviour
I fear looking like a failure if I don't achieve it...	I'm not putting in the effort that I could do to achieve the goal, I'm just drifting towards it...

It's also worth reflecting on whether *absolutely* everyone with a similar goal to you would have these fears? If they

49

didn't have these fears, how much more progress would they make than you towards the same goal?

Our adopted fears

When it comes to the crunch, many of us can tend to think, 'I want to achieve my goal but I can't just stop being afraid!'

It all sounds so simple in theory doesn't it ... when you are scared about something and you are getting bad results, you just decide to tell yourself that you were completely wrong to be scared, and all of a sudden your behaviour and results completely change. Hey presto!

Yeah, right! Try telling that to a petrified person who has been told to get up and speak in public. Research has actually shown that more people are afraid of public speaking than of death! You can't just *decide* that you aren't scared of it and make all of your fear magically disappear.

But are these fears innate in us, and therefore are we unable to stop them? Well the good news is that they are not, and therefore we *can* overcome fear.

To understand how we can learn to stop being afraid, we first need to understand how our brains work when it comes to fear. So, let's start at the beginning and see where these fears are actually coming from.

A common misconception:

It's often quoted that we *are* born with fears, albeit only two. These are a fear of the sensation of falling and a fear of loud noises. Interestingly, psychologists now believe that we aren't even born with these fears.

Psychologists now argue that instead of being born with these fears, we are in fact born with two reflexes that:

- Make us grasp when we experience the sensation of falling
- Make us jerk when we hear a loud noise.

These actions may be unconscious to begin with, but they connect to conscious fears as the infant matures and learns from the frightened reactions of others, such as their mother screaming in horror as the child falls. This latest interpretation of the research therefore indicates that *all* fears are in fact learned. They are literally man-made (or woman-made if we're talking about spiders). So, if all fears are learned, the next question to ask is: can they be unlearned? To answer this, we need to take a look at how the brain does what it does best: learn.

You will probably have heard of Pavlov's dogs. In his famous experiment, Pavlov sounded a bell prior to giving dogs food. At the sight of the food, the dogs would naturally salivate. Over time, however, the dogs came to realize that the food would always come when the bell was rung. Because of this, the dogs learned that the sound of the bell ringing and the delivery of the food were associated. The most important finding from this study was that ultimately just the sound of the bell was enough to make the dogs salivate – they didn't even need to see any food.

Joseph LeDoux is one of the world's leading researchers on the issue of how we learn fear. He explains that, just as Pavlov's dogs learned to associate two unrelated or neutral stimuli (i.e. a bell and food) if you experience fear at the same time as encountering a previously neutral stimulus, you can learn to associate that stimulus with fear.

Let's imagine you were bitten by your neighbour's dog yesterday. When you see it today – and for some time to come – the sight of it will likely trigger your 'flight, fight, or fright' response, which will either lead to you running away, preparing to do battle, or freezing dead in your tracks. These responses will all lead to a host of different physiological reactions.

What is key here are the words 'and for some time to come'. When Pavlov kept ringing the bell but stopped producing food, over time, the dogs learnt to disassociate the bell with the arrival of food. The response was 'unlearned'. Similarly, if you have repeated exposure to the dog that bit you, without mishap, after a while you can learn to no longer be afraid of it. 'Unlearning fear' is the basis for curing phobias.

So, although the thought of learning not to be afraid of something seems almost impossible, you can overcome your fears.

Undoing the fear

There are two key ways of learning to overcome fears, which are as follows ...

Behavioural therapy

If a person is afraid of dogs, a possible solution is to slowly bring that person more into contact with dogs, until they can learn to be relaxed with them. Initially, for example, this might involve having a dog in the room next door to them, visible through a closed glass door. The person will need to learn to be calm with the dog next door, through practicing relaxation techniques. In the next stage, the situation might be the same, except the person needs to learn to be relaxed whilst the door is open. Gradually, over time, the level of exposure to the dog will be increased until they can learn to be comfortable in close proximity to the dog.

Behavioural therapy works by indirectly challenging your beliefs about the dog. You may have started by feeling that the dog is terrifying. This feeling is never explicitly addressed. Instead you simply learn to get used to the dog and as a result are able to change your behaviour. This, over time, will alter your beliefs and you will come to realize that the dog isn't terrifying after all.

 Think of how you could use a behavioural therapy-style approach to overcoming some of your fears. For example, if your major goal is to educate as many people as possible on something you are passionate about, but one of your fears is of standing up in front of others and presenting, think about the incremental steps that you could take that would help you to get used to presenting.

Cognitive therapy

This involves reducing your level of fear through challenging and ultimately changing your beliefs about a certain situation. This is usually done through talking to another person who asks you questions about the matter. This method aims to directly challenge a belief that is causing you fear, trying to shake the foundations of your assumption that what you believe is real.

The **ABC model** is commonly used to structure a cognitive therapy intervention, originally developed by Albert Ellis in the 1950s.

A – stands for **Activating event** (what are the triggers that lead you to feel scared?)

B – stands for **Belief** (what are your assumptions about this situation?)

C – stands for **Consequence** (what feelings/behaviours/outcomes happen as a result of the activating event and the beliefs you have about it?).

If you don't like the results (consequences) that you are getting, it is helpful to go on to do steps D & E:

D – stands for **Dispute** (are there any other alternatives to this belief?)

E – stands for **Energizing alternative** (what would be a more empowering belief to adopt?).

 Think of how you could use the ABC (DE) model to overcome your goal-related fears.

Follow the steps to use the model as shown in the example below. Note the order here is ACBDE.

Step 1. What is the Activating event? E.g. I want a new job but am anxious about applying.

Step 2. What is the Consequence? E.g. I put off applying for jobs.

Step 3. What Belief underpinned that consequence? E.g. I'm no good at interviews.

Step 4. Is there any other way to interpret this situation that Disputes your belief? You can get better at interviews if you practice.

Step 5. What is an Energizing alternative belief to adopt? I should apply for a new job and I can improve my interview technique.

- Fears are responses to perceptions that our brain has associated with a threat.
- Behavioural therapy can enable you to unlearn a fear by breaking down the association.
- Cognitive therapy can help your brain think of different ways to evaluate an event, making your beliefs helpful rather than a hindrance.

 If our fears become an obstacle to us we can unlearn them as effectively as we adopted them.

G: Goals

A goal is a dream with a deadline.

Napoleon Hill

Have you ever lived by the mantra, 'just do your best'? If so, it turns out that you could be missing out on achieving your potential. If you want to achieve greater success, research has revealed that you should set yourself goals – and more precisely, that those goals should be specific and challenging, and that you should regularly monitor your progress towards achieving them.

See if you can identify with this: I decided to take up running and just tried to improve a bit. The results were pretty disastrous. I had never, in my entire life, run more than a mile and after several attempts I felt like I was literally dying after just trying to run for ten minutes (I'm not joking!). In the end, within only a month, I just gave up. Running was boring, painful and it didn't seem to be making any difference whatsoever to my fitness.

Whilst relaying my tale of 'running woe' to friends at a work summer party (and under the influence of a few too many glasses of Pimms), for some completely unknown reason, I boldly proclaimed, 'I'll run the marathon next year'. By the time I had woken up with a hangover the next morning, the news had spread like wildfire and people were coming up to me saying, 'Alison, I hear that you're running the marathon!' It was rather awkward and I found myself thinking, 'Well, I suppose I'd better do this then.'

Nine months later, after many hours of hard work, I completed the London Marathon in 5 hours and 50 minutes. It was one of the best days of my entire life. Interestingly, reflecting back I wonder if my finishing time would have been better if I hadn't said to myself, 'Just do your best, it's completing it that matters.' This episode in my life proved to me the enormous power of goal-setting, specifically:

- You can exceed your wildest dreams if you **set yourself a very challenging goal**. I can assure you that never in my wildest dreams, did I think that I would run a marathon. I used to watch it on television each year and think how much I would *love* to own a marathon medal (it was all about the medal!) but wonder how on earth people could run more than 3 miles.
- **Your goal should be specific**. I achieved far more when I was aiming to complete, say, a 5 km race during my training, than I did when I was just aiming to run as far as I could. Having something clear to aim for keeps you motivated when you feel like giving up and gives you a sense of pride when you complete it.
- **You should monitor your progress**. There was no way I could run 26.2 miles with no training. So I followed a training plan – I knew exactly what I had to do to be on track to complete the marathon. When I knew that

I was falling behind, this gave me focus to work harder
to achieve my targets.

The lessons of this story are backed up in the available
research. For example, leading experts Edwin Locke and
Gary Latham found that in over 90% of the studies that
they reviewed, setting a specific and challenging goal led
to superior performance compared to setting vague 'just
do your best' goals, or no goals at all.

They believe that, most fundamentally, goals direct
effort and attention. They also concluded that for goals
to be effective, people need feedback that measures their
progress in relation to the goal that they have set. If you
do not know how you are doing, it is impossible to adjust
the level or direction of your effort to match what the goal
requires.

Part 1

In the last few chapters we have begun to get
you thinking about a big, juicy goal! Now is
the time to get you to commit to achieving
that goal, and we can work on achieving it for the remainder of the book. So:

- Write down your goal, making it as specific as possible.
- Make sure that the thought of achieving it makes you
  feel really enthused.

- If you can, include a time limit (e.g. by 31st December this year).
- If you can, include a measure of success (e.g. 'having my own business with a turnover of £50,000 per year').

Part 2
- Find an envelope.
- Put the piece of paper with your goal written on it in the envelope. Be sure that you have noted down what your goal is elsewhere.
- Write the date that you intend to achieve the goal by on the outside of the envelope and write your address on the front.
- Ask someone (reliable!) in your life to keep your letter very safe and to post it to you on the date on the envelope.

Set short-term and long-term goals

We have seen above that goal-setting can be impactful in the long term, but it can also be a really effective daily strategy to utilize, as demonstrated by UCLA teacher Emily van Sonnenberg.

Emily was running a course in positive psychology and, as part of her course, she asked her students to complete a daily entry in what she calls an 'intention journal'. The daily entry consists of a 'specified daily goal' which is the answer to the question 'what do I want to achieve today?' Once their intention became clear, students were asked to record it in their journal.

Intentions could range from simple things such as making someone smile to more complex things, like improving how the student felt about themselves. At the end of the day, students were asked to review their progress towards their goal with a plus or minus symbol to show whether they'd accomplished it. At the end of the week, Emily asked the students to submit their journals for her to review. The purpose of this was two-fold: firstly, to hold students accountable for their own pursuit of goal-setting and secondly, to give students feedback about their goals, methods, and progress.

Each week Emily measured the students' achievements and concluded that, as Locke predicted, the students who set specific, difficult, but achievable goals which they believed were important, and who were also diligent about giving themselves feedback regarding their progress toward their goals, achieved their goals a staggering 92% more often than those students who set unspecific or easy goals and/or did not check in each night to record the progress they had made.

Goals are for life

Perhaps what is even more impressive than the statistic of achieving goals 92% more often, is the long term impact that carrying out this type of exercise can have.

Since she started running the class almost two years ago, Emily has received dozens of letters from her former students. She reports that each letter mentions how setting specific, difficult, but attainable goals that were important to them had become a way of life for the former student. This was due to the experience they had of such positive results after becoming disciplined to record intentions for themselves each day.

An even more significant result is the impact that using an intention journal has had on Emily's own life. She describes it as something that has 'worked wonders' for her. You see, five years ago Emily was involved in a car accident and came very close to death. As if that wasn't bad enough, the doctors told her she would never walk again. Not prepared to accept their diagnosis, she put in place her own disciplined goals in her intention journal. Through doing this, she regained her power to walk, against medical opinion.

If you have been inspired by Emily's story and the power of the 'specified daily goal', try this exercise:

- Sit quietly, relax and ask yourself the question 'What would I like to achieve today?'
- Write it down in your own Intention Journal.

- At the end of the day review whether you achieved your intention or not by drawing a smiley or a sad face.
- Repeat this every day, making intention-setting a way of life, and reap the benefits of this.

 Remember these, use them and you will reap the benefits of achieving your potential.

- Set goals – make them challenging.
- Make your goals specific.
- Review your progress towards your goals.
- Make goal-setting a habit.

 People who set specific and challenging goals are far more likely to achieve them than people who set only vague goals or no goals at all.

H: High

Shoot for the moon, even if you miss you will land amongst the stars.

Les Brown

You have just explored the power of goal-setting and specifically the principle of setting yourself a really **challenging goal**. Although people can generally see the benefits of this and can understand the reasoning behind it, they often still have concerns that they might have aimed too high.

It's only human to worry about failure and this is a common concern that many of us have. After all, if you set yourself a far too challenging goal, then you open yourself up to the very real possibility that you could fail. And if it's something that you *really* want and you put your heart and soul into achieving it, you experience the 'double whammy' of feeling extremely disappointed and looking stupid at the same time if you fail. You have to ask yourself, 'Why would I even bother?'

Rather than aiming high then, it might be safer to aim for average – if you achieve higher it's a bonus. There can even be a reluctance to aim high because, 'Where I am now is okay, thanks.'

So, let's look at the day of an average worker. You get woken up at hideous o'clock (when it's still dark) because it's time to get ready for work. You finally drag yourself out of bed when the snooze button can't be hit any more times or it will break. You become a zombie on the daily commute. You spend the next seven to eight hours (if you're lucky, that's all it is) on an emotional rollercoaster that can include fun but often involves stress or boredom. You leave work (it's now dark outside) and return to being a zombie on the commute home. You eat your dinner, clear up (if you can be bothered) and sit on the sofa. On goes the TV and you stare at the screen for a couple of hours before getting into bed, turning your alarm on and waiting for the day to start all over again.

Having worked with a lot of people we can confirm that, for some reason, people are very attached to this type of lifestyle. They resist taking action because it's 'okay as it is'. Just as we adapt to success in our lives, these people have adapted to the disappointment of a discomforting life and have buried their dreams with it.

Some people, some very successful people, don't accept this. Instead, they aim high and commit themselves to the task in hand. These people utilize a principle that Edwin Locke discovered in 1968: that there is a relation between the difficulty of the goal and the effort that is put into achieving it. Simply by aiming high, their performance rises to meet the occasion.

You can see this in effect when, in 1962, US President John F. Kennedy spoke of his desire to put a man on the moon. He announced, boldly:

We choose to go to the moon in this decade and do the other things, not because they are easy, but because they are hard, because that goal will serve to organize and measure the best of our energies and skills, because that challenge is one that we are willing to accept, one we are unwilling to postpone, and one which we intend to win.

In just this single public announcement, President Kennedy had committed the United States of America to putting a man on the moon before the end of the 1960s. He had told the whole nation that they were aiming high, so that it could respond accordingly, so that the performance of those who were involved would rise to the challenge.

And the result of this big, bold statement? As Neil Armstrong said in 1969, 'That's one small step for man ... one giant leap for mankind.'

 Look back at the description of the existence of the average worker described earlier. Your job is to give a school report-style grade to the existence described:

A – is for absolutely awesome, the best life could possibly be

B – is for good, it isn't perfect but it is reasonably close

C – is for average, a feeling of indifference, it could be better or worse

D – is for below average, definite room for improvement. Not awful

E – is for well below average, pretty bad, verging on awful

F – is for absolutely awful

How did you get on with that exercise? Let's imagine you rated this existence as grade C. Average, a feeling of indifference, it could be better or worse. People who are content with average, aim for average and as a result *get* average.

> *If you always do what you've always done, you'll always get what you've always got.*
>
> Susan Jeffries

Taking action opens new and unexpected doors

Remember Louise and the blue whale story? One thing is for certain – Louise was highly unlikely to ever see a blue whale while going about her everyday life. To achieve her dreams she had to take action. But what's interesting about taking action is the unexpected by-products that you can experience from trying something new.

Inspired by seeing the whale (who was nicknamed 'Eric'), Louise thought she might as well have a go at ticking off another goal on her list – 'find a man'. So, she joined an internet dating site. One month later, on her first date, she met her now-husband. They now have two pet goldfish. One is named Bubbles … the other is named Eric.

When you try new things in life, doors open to you, doors that you never knew existed or even thought to look for. Those doors can be practical, for example you might take action and find this leads to you meeting new people who you unexpectedly become friends with. Or they can be mental, changing your levels of confidence and your ability to try new things. These doors may or may not change your life in dramatic ways, but you will realize that when you step outside of your normal routine there are new experiences out there just waiting to be found. These experiences serve to make life richer – all because you aimed higher.

But what if I fail?

When people voice their concerns of experiencing failure, which they are using as reasons not to aim high, we share with them the inspirational quote from Les Brown at the beginning of this chapter: 'Shoot for the moon, even if you miss you will land amongst the stars.' It took a desperately disappointing week for me to understand the true value of these extremely wise words.

In the last chapter I described my story of running the London Marathon. Although everything turned out all right in the end, this very nearly wasn't the case.

It was just 6 days before the big day and, after months of training in the cold, my poor hands were looking rather chapped and sore. My mother kindly lent me some hand cream that I had bought her as a birthday present and I enjoyed the soothing sensation of the cream on my hands (good choice of present!).

When I woke up the next day, I noticed a nasty red mark on the back of my left hand. Thinking that my hands really had suffered in the cold, I generously slapped some more of the luxurious cream on the mark.

Over the following few hours, I realized that I was having a severe allergic reaction to the hand cream. We have talked about believing in the impossible – I had never before believed that my hand could swell up to the size of a boxing glove! The red mark had now turned into an enormous, disgusting blister. And to make matters far worse (apologies for the gory details), I started throwing up. And throwing up. And throwing up some more. Every time I tried to swallow something to calm my stomach, it came straight back up. Eating was totally out of the question, which is absolutely not recommended in the final days of preparation to run a marathon.

The following day I went to the doctor, who told me that my allergic reaction had caused a severe infection in my body. She gave me antibiotics and told me that if I did not stop vomiting within 24 hours I would have to be admitted to hospital.

The pressure on me to pull out from the marathon was immense. Everyone kept saying that I was nowhere near well enough to run. After months of totally dedicated training I was absolutely gutted at the prospect of having to withdraw. One of the things that kept going through my mind was what a failure I would be. Everyone knew that I was running the marathon – my sister had even flown over from her home in California especially to watch me. I had raised over £2,500 for charity and I was facing the very real prospect of falling at the last hurdle.

I can totally identify with the downsides of shooting for the moon and aiming way outside of your comfort zone. It does indeed open you up to the very possibility that you will not succeed. When you have articulated your dream or goals to others, you feel an immense pressure to live up to the expectation that you have created. When you have put all of your energy and focus into achieving something and have come so close to succeeding, the thought of starting all over again is devastating. You feel like all of your hard work has been wasted.

Recognize your successes

So would everything have been wasted if I couldn't run the marathon?

In my hours of disappointment I was unable to see that simply by shooting for the moon, I had succeeded way beyond my previous capabilities. During my training, I had completed a twenty-mile race, therefore I had run at least nineteen miles further than I could run before I tried. I realized very poignantly from this that the only way you can really fail is if you never try at all.

Thankfully, the antibiotics worked and my doctor gave me permission to run the marathon. But this episode taught me an extremely valuable lesson in life. Les Brown's words, 'even if you miss you will land amongst the stars', are so very true.

 Reflect on this for a few minutes: is there something that you *really* want in life, but that just seems too challenging to even try?

Allow yourself to daydream a little about what you really want in your life now, or recall what it used to be that you really wanted that you don't yet have.

What has been holding you back from achieving it?

Would you rather be a failure for attempting to achieve it, or a failure for not attempting to achieve it at all?

- Be bold in your goal-setting – don't be afraid to aim high.
- If you don't take part in the right level of challenge you can't succeed.
- Recognize that the outcome isn't everything – there are successes along the way too.

IF YOU REMEMBER ONE THING If you aim for average you'll get average, so aim high and get the reward your potential deserves.

Achieving 65% of the impossible is better than 100% of the ordinary. Setting impossible goals and achieving part of them sets you on a completely different path than the safe route.

Dan Dodge, Google

I: Interim steps

The secret to getting ahead is getting started.
The secret to getting started is breaking your complex,
overwhelming tasks into small manageable tasks, and
then starting on the first.

Mark Twain

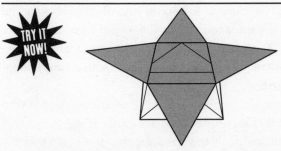

Find a square of paper, approximately 20×20 cm. Your task is to make the origami box shown above.

So how did you get on with making your own box? What do you mean you can't do it?

This box may look overwhelmingly complicated to make, but in reality it's just a sequence of simple folds, carried out in the right order. The secret to making the box is focusing on achieving one step at a time, breaking the complex whole down into a series of simple baby steps.

You will find the instructions at **www.the-psychology-of-success.com/origami-instructions** if you want to impress your friends and family with your origami folding skills!

This box is a representation of your goal. It may appear complex on the face of it, so to succeed you need to break the goal down into a series of manageable steps and know the order you need to complete them in.

Have an action plan

Professor of Psychology at New York University, Peter Gollwitzer, has found that people who plan in advance the steps that will be taken to achieve a goal (including when, where and how action will be taken), achieve greater success. Gollwitzer calls the plan that you create an **implementation intention**.

Professor Gollwitzer's research shows that people who use implementation intentions are more likely to achieve large, ambitious goals than people who do not set them.

Implementation intentions also help you to achieve smaller goals too. For example, it has been shown that the number of healthy foods (i.e. fruit and vegetables) a person eats can easily be increased if they are asked to form implementation intentions on what they will eat for the different meals of a given day. So now you know what to do if you want to reach your 'five a day' target!

Another reason that breaking your goals down into baby steps helps you to succeed is that it helps you to believe that you can do it.

For example, the goal, 'I want to be able to run the London Marathon, in less than four hours, next year,' is very daunting, whereas the task of going to a running shop and selecting the right footwear for running is relatively easy.

The breaking down of goals into manageable steps is something that has been used successfully for years. At the 1972 Olympics held in Munich, Mark Spitz won seven gold medals for swimming, breaking an impressive seven world records on the way.

17-year-old John Naber was so impressed by Mark's achievements he set himself the goal of winning the gold in the 100 metres backstroke at the next Olympics in 1976. However, John's current personal best was only 59.5 seconds, compared to the winning time of 56.3 seconds.

John realized that he was going to have to do better than that, so set himself a target of 55.5 seconds (notice that's a specific and measurable goal). If he was going to achieve this time (which would be a world record) he would have to go four seconds faster over the next four years. So, to break it down, that's one second per year he needed to improve by. Because swimmers train for about ten months a year, he divided that goal of one second each year down to 1/10th of a second each month.

John didn't stop there. He worked out that as he trained six days a week, that broke it down to 1/300th of a second a day. And then he took it even further: he trained for four hours a day – that made it 1/1200th of a second each hour. To put that into context, if you blink your eyes, the time it takes them to close is 5/1200ths of a second. Now, doesn't his ambitious dream now sound like a realistic goal?

While John may initially have aimed high, setting himself a goal he didn't believe he could achieve, by breaking it down into the smallest of measurable steps he was able to make sure he had a path to achieve his end goal.

And the result of his implementation intention? He won the gold in both the 100 metres and the 200 metres backstroke, the first in world record time (55.49 seconds) and the second in Olympic record time. He had made what seemed impossible to him very much possible and achieved his dream of holding an Olympic gold medal.

Believe in your ability

This relates to a well known theory in psychology called **self-efficacy**, a term coined by Albert Bandura in 1977. Self-efficacy is a person's belief in his or her ability to succeed in a given situation.

'I am the greatest', I said that even before I knew I was.
Muhammad Ali

People with strong self-efficacy are more likely to achieve their goals than people with weak self-efficacy, who will likely avoid challenging tasks, believing them to be beyond their capabilities.

One of the benefits of breaking your goals down into manageable chunks is that even a person with low self-efficacy can achieve tasks and work towards a major goal, because the smaller tasks are not so daunting.

Have a go at beginning to develop your own implementation intention plan, to support you to achieve your goal. Here's what to do:

- Grab three pads of Post-it notes, all different colours, say yellow, green and orange.
- On the green Post-it note write your major goal. Make it specific and measurable (e.g. 'I want to have my own business, earning at least as much money as I do now through my current job, within three years.').
- On the yellow Post-it notes brainstorm all of the things that you need to do to achieve your goal (e.g. 'think of a company name'; 'buy a website'; 'produce marketing fliers'; 'get business cards'; 'find my first client'; 'open a business bank account'; 'get professional indemnity insurance'; etc.).
- Now, sort all of your yellow Post-it notes into themes of related items. For example, 'buy a website', 'produce marketing fliers' and 'get business cards' might go in a cluster under 'marketing'.
- Next, put the Post-it notes in order of when you need to achieve them. Your aim is to create a line of Post-it notes that stretches from the first action that you need to take, all the way to the green Post-it note at the end.

- Finally, look at the date that you have set for yourself to achieve the end goal and, using the orange Post-it notes, make a timeline by putting dates next to your actions (e.g. the first action might have a Post-it note saying 'tomorrow' next to it).

- Seemingly impossible or complex goals can be achieved one step at a time.
- Make your implementation intention specific and measurable.
- Believe that you have the ability to achieve each step of the action plan and the end goal.

In order to achieve your goal, break down the activities you will need to do to complete it, put them in the order needed, then begin with the first.

J: Just have a go!

The man who makes no mistakes does not usually make anything.

Edward John Phelps

You may know people who have hopes and dreams but frustratingly, never do anything about them. To put it another way, they procrastinate, which University of Calgary lecturer Piers Steel defines as 'voluntarily delaying an intended course of action despite expecting to be worse off for the delay'.

Perhaps you are procrastinating over something that you want. If so, read on.

Why do we procrastinate?

Psychologists such as Barbara Fritz at the University of Florida are fascinated by the question of what makes us procrastinate. It has been concluded that there are two key reasons we do.

One reason is **fear of failure** – we are worried that we aren't going to do the task particularly well and so put it off and prefer to do things we are 'better' at (such as watching television or playing football).

The other main reason is labelled **task aversion**, or to put this in a non-jargon way – we hate doing it because it's an awful bind compared with something more enjoyable (such as watching television or playing football!).

Why do we have a fear of failure?

Have you ever seen parents trying to coach their toddler to walk? What is their reaction when Junior takes his first steps and falls right over on his bottom? Do Mum and Dad yell in rage? Of course not – they cheer! Junior just walked!

So what goes wrong? Somewhere between learning to walk and becoming an adult, instead of being encouraged to try and being rewarded for trying even though we failed, we somehow are taught that we must get it right first time.

For example, at work we avoid giving presentations, fearing that we will look stupid. Or perhaps we are just scared of taking the wrong decision and making a mistake. To avoid being punished, we procrastinate and hope that someone else will act instead.

Yet the fact of the matter is that no toddler ever got up and walked perfectly for ten minutes on the first attempt. No teenager ever got into a car and drove faultlessly for 100 miles first time. We fall, we stall and that is the way that it has to be in order for us to learn.

Overcoming the fear of failure

Key to the psychology of success is how you view failure. Once you've accepted the principle that you have to try in order to succeed, the next key steps are to:

- Find ways to see a failure as a good result
- Re-label failure as a learning opportunity.

Don't worry about failure, worry about the chances
you miss when you don't even try.

Harvey Mackay

Why do we suffer from task aversion?

Many, many people will be able to identify with the feeling of desperately wanting to get in shape but still not having enough motivation to get up early and go to the gym.

At the heart of this is the fact that we think of things like going to the gym as painful. When you have the choice of getting up (while it is still dark, yuck!) and dragging yourself to the gym before work or else having an extra hour in your warm cosy bed, it isn't really a difficult choice is it? Getting up is painful; staying tucked up under the duvet is pleasurable.

We therefore associate taking action with pain and not taking action with pleasure, hence we don't act. But what implication does this have?

A friend of ours, Becky, had been in a relationship for nine years and was engaged to be married. The wedding was all arranged but one day she uttered the words, 'I just don't feel the same about him.' In the next sentence she said, 'But I can't call the wedding off, it's too difficult.'

Becky was, however, sensible enough to take a longer term view. Yes, calling off the wedding would be pretty horrendous and there was some minor relief associated with not having to tell her partner, his family and all of their acquaintances about how she felt, and not having to confront the enormous waste of money. However, Becky realized that although she was seeing it as a case of '**pain if I act, pleasure if I don't**', in the long term it was far more sensible to think, '**pleasure if I act, pain if I don't**', thus avoiding spending years trapped in an unhappy marriage.

So, the associations of whether we view something as painful or pleasurable in the long term are key. Going back to the cold, dark morning, if you put off going to the gym every day, taking a longer term view you could well face a situation where there are far more painful consequences as a result of being in poor physical condition than simply getting out of bed would have caused!

Overcome the problem of task aversion

It's very difficult to convince yourself that going to the gym is pleasurable. After all, look at that warm, fluffy duvet – how can it not win every time!

Clearly the most sensible way to overcome this is to find a type and time of exercise that you actually enjoy. Remember Chapter C (current vs. future) – this is, after all, following the principle of enjoying the journey *and* the destination.

However, there may be times when it isn't possible to change the task that you need to do: it's something that just has to be done in order to reach your goal. If that is the case, perhaps we can learn a handy tip from Harvard's Positive Psychology Lecturer, Shawn Achor.

Shawn talks about the principle of **activation energy**. In chemistry, activation energy describes the relatively large amount of energy that it takes to start a chemical reaction. However, once a reaction has begun, less energy is needed to sustain it. Think of a rocket that's taking off to the moon – it has to use a large amount of fuel to beat gravity, but once it's up there, soaring in the air, it needs far less power to travel.

You may well be able to identify with the thought that exercise is pretty terrible, but once you actually start exercising, you find it's quite enjoyable. So, Shawn Achor's learned advice to us procrastinators is to decrease the activation energy required to complete a task.

Shawn describes how he wanted to go out running first thing in the morning, but he too was finding it too much effort (who can blame him!). The solution: for several weeks, he went to sleep in his running shorts and t-shirt, with his socks and shoes beside his bed. He only had to get up in the morning, put his shoes and socks on and leave the house – he decreased the amount of effort required to get started. He advocates this strategy as a very effective way to overcome procrastination. We can testify what a useful strategy this is – several of the chapters of this book have been written whilst wearing running kit!

Finally, sometimes we find that we spend so mu~~c~~ time just thinking about how much we don't want something, that it actually would have been quicker just to do it! If you feel like you are procrastinating, it's well worth asking yourself, 'Would you just be better taking immediate action now?'

The surest way to beat procrastination, and to save yourself from wasting the time worrying about it, is just to get on with doing whatever you are avoiding.

 The world is full of people with hopes and dreams that they never did anything about. Do you want to be one of them? If not, right now, take decisive action towards completing the first step of the action plan that you created in the previous chapter.

Ask yourself, 'What is the most important thing that I need to do to begin to achieve the first step of my action plan?'

Use any resources you want – phone, internet, speaking to someone, looking up a phone number, anything that will help you. The most important thing is to take action right now to make your dream start to come true.

If you don't try you will never succeed. Just have a go. You may well surprise yourself.

As you get older in life, you will find that the only things
that you regret are the things that you didn't do.
Zachary Scott

- You can't achieve anything by just thinking about it, you have to take action as well.
- If we're procrastinating it's because we fear failure or we're avoiding the task.
- Overcome fear of failure by remembering that you can only learn if you try.
- Overcome task aversion by remembering that there will be more pain in the future for you if you don't act than there is pain for you today if you do.

IF YOU REMEMBER ONE THING Nothing will hold you back more than not doing anything to achieve your goal, so take action, and whenever you find yourself not moving forward with your goal, take immediate action then too!

K: Keep going

Fall down seven times, stand up eight.
Japanese proverb

Thomas Edison, the prolific inventor and famed creator of the light bulb, is often cited in stories about persevering until you succeed. Indeed, having apparently made over 1,000 attempts to create the light bulb, he is testament to the argument that you should keep going even when you fail, because you only need to succeed once to succeed.

Consider the impact on our current way of life if Edison had given up (especially given the fact that you may currently be reading this with the help of an electric light bulb).

I have not failed. I've found 1,000 ways that won't work.
Thomas Edison

However, perhaps more interesting is to look at some of the earlier events in Thomas Edison's life. Edison didn't even talk until he was 4 years old and developed hearing problems from an early age, eventually leading him to become almost totally deaf. He was not allowed to start school until he was 7 due to having been born with a peculiar physical appearance and suffering from a bout of scarlet fever. Even then, he had only three months of formal school education, after his teacher lost patience with his hyperactivity.

Thomas was always curious, a trait demonstrated by his experimentation with fire (which led to him burning down the family barn). But he channelled this curiosity into inventing. Even then, it was not a smooth ride. His first patented invention, an electronic vote counter, was a disaster because there was no demand for it. As a young man, he found himself deeply in debt and without money for food. And, in 1879, he just missed out to Alexander Graham Bell, who beat Edison to become the first person to patent the authentic transmission of the human voice in the form of the telephone.

Yet despite all of these setbacks Thomas Edison became one of the greatest inventors of all time. How did he keep going? Early research by Martin Seligman, founder of the field of positive psychology, can shed light on why some people can keep going despite repeated failure.

In a rather distasteful study, conducted a long time before positive psychology was invented, Seligman and his colleagues studied the impact that electric shocks had on the behaviour of a group of dogs.

In the first part of the experiment, the dogs received electric shocks but had no ability whatsoever to stop them. After a while the dogs simply gave up trying to turn the shocks off and became passive, displaying depression.

In the second part of the experiment, again the dogs experienced electric shocks, however this time they could escape them with just a simple jump over a barrier. Despite the ease with which they could escape the pain they were receiving, the dogs again just sat down and whimpered – they had learned to be helpless.

However, what initially annoyed Seligman (but eventually became the making of some fascinating psychological research), was the fact that approximately 1 in 3 dogs never learned to be helpless and continued to look for a way to escape the electric shocks.

Just as the dogs differed in their ability to bounce back from a difficult situation, so too can we humans.

THINK ABOUT IT Of your close friends and family, who is an example of someone who becomes despondent and gives up easily in the face of failure? Conversely, who do you know who has great levels of 'bounce back ability' and seems to be resilient in difficult circumstances?

Where does failure lie?

Thomas Edison was reputed to have a strong ability to persevere and even as a child he was willing to keep going, no matter what. This behaviour served him well in his profession as an inventor. So what is it that determines whether we give up or keep going? Psychologists believe that this is related to the way that we interpret a situation when we fail.

For example, take two people, Barbie and Cindy, who are looking to meet their ideal partners. They've decided that they've had enough of being single and so have each gone on the internet to find a boyfriend. For four weeks, both have been on the same dating website and have met a few boys. Unfortunately, none of the dates have gone well and neither has met the right person for them.

However, when their ex-boyfriends, Ken and Paul, ask the girls how their search is going, they give very different responses. Barbie admits that she hasn't found anyone yet but says that she is going to try a new dating website instead, because she doesn't think that the one that she tried was very good for meeting the kind of person she is interested in. In contrast, Cindy wants to give up because she has learned that meeting a date over the internet simply doesn't work.

In this example Barbie is seeing the setback as temporary. Sure, this approach to dating didn't work this time, but that doesn't mean another website can't provide what she's looking for. In contrast, Cindy is reading the failed dates as representative of all internet dating and so dismissing the idea completely without trying elsewhere.

It's always too early to quit.
Norman Vincent Peale

So, the explanations we make about the events we experience impact on how we act in the face of failure. The explanations that we make are linked to our way of thinking.

One way to change how you're thinking about failure is to become more consciously aware of the way that you think and behave. For example, if you find that you give up easily when things go wrong, start to ask yourself why. Try to uncover the belief that is making you give up – in Cindy's case it is the belief that 'internet dating doesn't work'.

It is always critical to remember that a belief is a belief and *not* reality. If you don't like the outcome you're getting, for example you are failing to meet your ideal partner online, it is always worth trying to question whether everyone has that experience or whether others have proved that this type of dating does work. Try to shake the foundation of your negative belief.

If you want it enough you'll keep going

As a child, Walter told his dad that he dreamt of being an artist, but in Walter's own words, 'My father didn't buy that.' Despite this cynicism, Walter persisted and launched his career as an artist and began experimenting by making cartoons. Even with a lot of hard work, sadly Walter's efforts did not pay off and at the age of just 23 he was declared bankrupt. In the face of adversity, a brave Walter set off for Hollywood with barely more than $40, a paintbrush and a pair of trousers. With nothing more to lose, Walter went into business with his also-unemployed brother Roy, and thankfully things started to turn around.

The brothers had their first commercial success with *Oswald the Lucky Rabbit*, but just as things were looking up, their world came crashing down. They lost ownership of Oswald and many of the artists working for them to the distributor of the cartoon, because of a contract loophole.

After this betrayal, Walter remained resolute, and with the one remaining artist who had stayed loyal to him, created a new animation based on a pet he had adopted. Mickey Mouse was born, and Walt(er) Disney began creating the legacy of Disney characters we know today.

> *All the adversity I've had in my life, all my troubles and*
> *obstacles, have strengthened me ... You may not realize*
> *it when it happens, but a kick in the teeth may be the*
> *best thing in the world for you.*
>
> Walt Disney

 Think of a time when you attempted to do something and it didn't work out for you.

- What did you think the reason you did not succeed was at that time?
- If you tried to do the same thing again, did you try as hard, if not harder?
- If you did not try to do the same again, why was that?
- What would need to have happened differently for you to have succeeded?
- Are there any other ways you could have approached it and succeeded?

- What have you learnt about how you come to think of failure in these situations?
- How would you like to feel if you had tried but not yet succeeded?

- When we don't have control over a situation we just let it happen, so take back control.
- Every experience of failure you have is another way to help you find success.
- If you really want something, you'll find new ways to keep pushing through the obstacles you come across.

 Just because you haven't succeeded yet, doesn't mean that you won't.

L: Learn

Whenever you fall, pick something up.
                                        Oswald Avery

Imagine you have set yourself the goal of learning to juggle. You are fired up to succeed and you aren't satisfied with juggling just two balls, so you go for three! The fear of dropping the ball has been overcome (yes, people really do stand frozen, psyching themselves up to make that first throw!). You've broken your goal down into steps and you have even taken the first step and thrown the balls. And where did they land? Perfectly in your hands first time? We think not!

This happens all the time when trying to achieve goals. When you try something new, particularly when it's challenging, the balls all land straight on the floor with a big old thud! You failed! L-o-o-o-ser!

If you have ever watched a group of adults trying to learn how to juggle, the psychology of their behaviour is really fascinating. Some wannabe jugglers seem motivated to succeed and keep going. Others get more and more frustrated. When you watch the frustrated people, it is quite amusing (harsh but true) to see them make the same mistakes over and over again. They simply whinge that they are 'no good at juggling', and, 'I can't do it, what's the point in even trying?'

What is interesting about these people is that rather than being no good at juggling, they are no good at *learning*. If you continue to throw the ball in the same way over and over again, it's always going to land on the floor. Trying to throw the balls is critical, but so is learning from your mistakes.

> *The definition of insanity is doing the same thing over and over again and expecting a different result.*
> Albert Einstein

Can you stop yourself from dropping the balls?

We've almost certainly all experienced that horrifying moment when you press the 'save' button on your computer and realize that you have accidentally saved over something that you spent hours working on. All of your hard work is gone. Crushing.

While writing one of the chapters in this book, we were highly successful at doing exactly that. There is that moment of calmness, 'Surely I didn't do that?' Followed by the cringe-worthy confirmation that yes you really *did* just do that. Next comes the obligatory panic-stricken search, which sometimes ends in relief in the form of an auto-saved file. For us it didn't end so well.

When you have goals, from buying a new house to writing a book, mistakes happen. Things go wrong. No matter how careful you are, or how much you plan or try, you can't avoid them. Even if you have been really careful, there are a million things that could go wrong. So what is critical is how you react when things do fail. Here are some techniques to use so that you always 'pick something up when you fall'.

1: Ask yourself, 'What's the silver lining?'

They say that every rain-laden, stormy-black cloud has a silver lining, and asking yourself the question, 'What's the silver lining?' can certainly help you to find it. In the instance of the deleted chapter, the answer to that question was, 'At least it was only one chapter and not the whole book.'

Though we had made a mistake, something very positive came out of this negative situation. We immediately went and backed up the entire book onto a memory stick – the chances of losing the book were then far slimmer.

2: Failure can help you to achieve better long-term results

Let's take a situation where you are good at your job but need to develop and grow from what you're currently doing. Because there have been no internal opportunities available, you decide to interview with other companies. The only problem is, you haven't interviewed since you got this job and you're quite rusty at it.

So, when you go on your first interview and you don't get invited back to the second round, you take it a bit personally. They had thought you were right on paper, but clearly something was not right when they met you. Now, rather than taking that as a sign that you should stay in the company and role you have, the best approach would be to learn from that. Did you convey your strengths in your answers? Was the conversation positive? Did you ask the right questions? Did you get the right answers? Based on what you found out from them in the interview, would it have been the right company for you anyway? If so, why was that?

Getting the answers to these questions would help you to develop your interviewing skills in the longer term, helping you shine at interviews, and ensuring that you get a good fit between what the company wants and what you have to offer.

3: Ask yourself, 'What do I want instead of what I have now?'

It can be very tempting to dwell on failure when it happens and wallow in the negative emotions that it can bring. If we are completely truthful, there is something really quite cathartic about the experience of moaning and reaping the resulting sympathy from our friends and family.

What is critical to realize however, is that this doesn't actually get you anywhere. Your time could be much better spent trying to do something to change the situation, rather than spending it complaining about it or contemplating it. By focusing on what you want, and not on what you have right now, you can make a lot of progress.

4: Remember that you have more to become

When you were a baby you couldn't walk, let alone read. When you were a child, you yearned to be able to drive, but the first time you got behind the wheel we bet you weren't quite ready for Formula One stardom. When you started your first job, we bet you didn't have the knowledge and the skills that you do now. Appreciate that your talents, your abilities and even your intelligence, are not things that are set in stone. These have grown over time and will continue to do so.

5: Remember that you learned through the experience of trying

You will probably be able to identify with the fact that doing the same piece of work a second time around is actually far quicker than when you tried it the first time. This is because your brain has already done a lot of the thinking and learning about how to do it. So, for example, while rewriting that chapter of your book takes up some more of your time, it also gives you the opportunity to write it better the second time round.

 Think of a time when you haven't been able to achieve your goal:

- What has been positive about this experience?

- How did this help you to understand how better to approach the goal?
- Rather than what you ended up with, what was it that you had wanted to achieve?
- What has this experience shown that you need to develop further in yourself?
- If you had to attempt this goal again, what have you learnt that would help you to better achieve it second time around?

Write each of your answers down.

You only need as much intelligence as a squirrel

Finally, you should take inspiration from the humble squirrel that appeared in a Carling Black Label beer television commercial a few years ago. Accompanied by the theme tune from *Mission Impossible*, our friend the squirrel negotiated a tough obstacle course, which included leaping accurately across gaps of many feet. There's no way that the squirrel could have completed the course without making many mistakes to reach his goal. In fact, the film crew were there for days, waiting for the squirrel to complete the course. So remember, it's always worth the effort to reach those nuts!

- When you make a mistake, always try to find the valuable lesson it teaches you and, critically, take action to implement that lesson.
- Through failing you can be far more successful in the long term, as it makes you focus. You will also have learnt a valuable lesson that might stop you making the same mistakes again.
- When things go wrong, it is critical to think how your precious time and energy might be best spent to get you to where you want to be.
- When we fail at something, it can mean that we haven't yet developed the ability to achieve it, so keep on developing yourself.
- The fruits of your efforts won't all have been lost if you fail. You learned through the experience of trying and you may well be closer to succeeding as a result.

Nobody's perfect – everybody makes mistakes and fails. To be successful you have to accept that this will happen and then learn from these failures.

M: Modelling

Success leaves clues.

Anthony Robbins

In the previous chapter, we explored how it's sometimes critical to fail in order to succeed. You have to learn through your mistakes. But wouldn't it be good if there was a short-cut to learning how to do something? Well there is and that shortcut is called **modelling**. This doesn't mean that you have to put on a bikini and walk down a catwalk (unless you want to, of course!). It is to do with the concept of having a role model to copy.

When it comes to success stories we all have a ready supply of examples that we can roll off the tongue. From sportspeople to entrepreneurs, politicians to film stars, friends and family, there are already many people around us who have achieved exactly the goals we want to achieve.

The good news for you is that, because these success stories exist, it puts you one step closer to achieving your own success. Why? Because whatever it is you are seeking to achieve, the likelihood is that someone else has already put in the hours of trial and effort, working out what works and what doesn't (i.e. learning from their mistakes). They've now got what they were looking for and have the t-shirt to prove it. And the best thing is that very often people will happily pass on their wisdom to somebody who desires much the same thing as they did.

Learning from others has been around as long as humans have walked the planet. In psychology, how we go about learning from others has been made popular through the work of Albert Bandura and his experiments conducted in the 1970s.

In one such experiment, that formed the basis for his theory on social learning, Bandura divided a group of young boys and girls from a nursery school. Individually, the children would go into a playroom where there were toys and an inflatable Bobo doll, a cheery-looking clown. In each case, an adult walked into the room and played on their own with the toys for a minute, with the child watching. The adult would then either give kind attention to Bobo for the remainder of their time in the room *or* take the toys and start to administer the clown with a good whacking.

Now, when the adult left the room, all eyes were on the behaviour of the children. Those who had seen the adult play gently with the clown followed suit, giving it the same loving, playful attention. However, the children who had seen the adult treat Bobo badly made a different choice. They played with the toys alright, but only using them as weapons to administer their own brand of a thumping to the poor clown. In fact, the children in this group were even more creative in their tormenting of Bobo than the adult, using toys the adult hadn't used, pinning Bobo down and smacking him with a toy hammer.

Crucially, it's because the children observed and learned what it was possible to do that they conceived that they could also do it. Both groups of children, those who were kind to Bobo and those who beat him, had the capability to display either set of behaviour. The choice of which they did display was a result of the role model.

Similarly, you have the capability and resources you need to achieve the goals you have set yourself. Having the right role model to learn from – and then actually learning from them – can prove very beneficial in making your goal become a reality.

 Take a few minutes to think about your family, friends and acquaintances. Who is your role model for each of the following?

- Good health
- Adventurous spirit
- Generosity/altruism/kindness
- Wisdom
- Open-mindedness
- Love
- Bravery
- Forgiveness

What are the behaviours or attitudes of each of the role models you identified that you could learn to model?

We are even wired up to learn from others

In the early 1990s, Italian researcher Giacomo Rizzolatti and his colleagues were conducting a routine study of the electrical activities of macaque monkeys' brains when they made a fascinating discovery.

Their aim had been to observe the resulting activity in a monkey's brain when it made various movements, such as grasping for a peanut or cracking it open. The researchers had therefore hooked up a series of electrodes to the monkey's head and were monitoring the monkey's movements and the resulting brain activity.

The researchers expected to see brain activity when the monkey moved. However, astonishingly, they found readings from the electrodes were occurring as if the monkey was grasping for a peanut, when in fact it was sitting motionless.

The baffled researchers suddenly realized that the monkey's neurons had fired in response to seeing one of the researchers grasp for his own food. Neurons were firing whether the monkey moved or saw someone else move. **Mirror neurons** had been discovered. But what on earth is a mirror neuron?

A regular neuron is a cell that transmits signals around your body, informing it what to do. It helps the decision-making part of your body, the brain, communicate with the body parts that carry out the actions, such as your fingers. So if we tell you to put this book down and pick it up again, your brain processes that, then transmits an impulse through neurons to the muscles in your arm so that you carry out the action. Those impulses can be measured by a scientist and were what they were studying in the monkey eating peanuts.

A mirror neuron is a special type of neuron, which doesn't fire when you are doing a task, but instead fires when you see someone else doing a task. So the monkey's mirror neurons were firing when it saw the scientist reach for his own food. It's because of mirror neurons that when we smile at babies, they smile back at us. It's also why football fans, when watching a game on TV, will imitate heading the ball when they see their star player getting ready to do the same to score a goal.

Using modelling for success

In 1984, Dr Wyatt Woodsmall and a group of trainers were invited by the US Army to trial a new pistol-firing training program amongst its soldiers. The army's current training program was four days long and had a pass rate of 70%. Dr Woodsmall's task was to improve the shooting ability of the soldiers at a faster rate than the current program.

Dr Woodsmall's team set about learning the different approaches to firing a pistol and the precise techniques used by studying the best marksmen around. These expert marksmen would have fired shots thousands upon thousands of times, adjusting their technique and developing their skill until they were recognized as excelling in this field. They were tested to find out what helped them to perform at their best, and also what detracted from their abilities. Their techniques were then taken and adapted to form the new training program.

When the new training program was ready, a group of participating soldiers was split into two teams. The first team received the standard training program and the second team received the new program that was based on modelling the techniques used by the experts, who had already learned by trial and error.

For a solider to pass and be given the grade of Marksman he would have to get 30 hits on target out of 45 rounds fired. The first group, using the traditional training, received 27 hours of training, with just over 70% of the soldiers passing the test and receiving the grade of Marksman.

The second group, trained by Dr Woodsmall's team, undertook just twelve hours of training. The result? 100% of the soldiers passed and were graded as Marksman – impressive! In less than half the time these novice shooters were able to achieve better results by using the tried and tested techniques of the best shooters around. In fact, 25% of these previously inexperienced shooters, after just twelve hours of training, had developed beyond the Marksman grade and were being awarded the rank of Expert.

Identify someone in your network, or an acquaintance of someone in your network, and ask them if you could learn from them by observing them in a specific situation. You'll be surprised just how keen some people are to help when you ask them – it can be flattering to be asked, after all.

As an example of the above, our friend Liz lost a staggering 6.5 stone in just six months, dropping from a UK size 20 to size 12. She was more than happy to share the tips of her success. She said her strategy was to have a high protein diet, combined with six weekly trips to the gym, two 1-hour sessions of doing weights and four 5 km runs on the treadmill per week.

What was also interesting was the psychological boost that this gave Liz. She said that it was hard at first but then, as she started seeing results, she began to love the challenge. As well as modelling a person's skills or strategies, you can model a person's beliefs too. Liz proves that, contrary to what we were saying earlier, it's possible to be both very successful at weight loss and to enjoy it! Now Liz is just on a weight maintenance diet but she still loves going to the gym four times a week.

If you get the results you're looking for first time, well done, you've modelled successfully. If you don't, then don't worry; you're learning how best to do something new and practice makes perfect. Remember to reward yourself for your efforts, no matter how small the reward is.

One thing to make sure of is that you have the right 'recipe' (the mix of steps, actions or behaviours the other person performs) from your observations. So do check back and seek further clarification or mentoring from the person who you modelled on, until you can achieve your goal.

- The achievements of others are an invaluable resource for you – other people may already possess the abilities you need to achieve your goal.
- By modelling another's pattern for success you will be able to create a recipe for your own success.
- The choice of your role model is very important, as you will come to believe that you are capable of the behaviour that they display.

 We can improve our ability to realize our goals by tapping into the abilities and behaviours of people who have experienced success in the same area.

N: Numbers

You have to know where you stand and where you want to go,
or else it isn't going to happen. Numbers bring clarity.
                                                    Subir Chowdhury

Deep in the forests of America in the 1970s, two groups of loggers were hard at work under the eagle eye of psychologist Gary Latham. Latham's quest was to work out what would influence the loggers to cut down more trees.

Both groups of loggers were treated identically except for one key aspect. The first group were simply told to do their best and cut down as many trees as possible. In contrast, the second group were taught how to calculate the theoretical maximum number of trees that they could fell and were given a counter to wear on their belts so they could keep track of their progress towards that goal.

After twelve weeks of felling and counting trees, the 'goal-setting' group had felled significantly more trees than the group told to try as hard as they could.

From this study and many others, goal-setting gurus Latham and his colleague Locke concluded that getting feedback on your progress towards a goal, through regular measurement, is a powerful strategy to increase achievement. We talked about this in chapter 'G' when exploring the power of goal-setting; however, as this is such an important concept, we are now going to explore it in more detail.

So why does feedback on our progress improve success rates? There are various reasons; here are a few of them:

1. We can't emphasize enough the fabulous feeling you will experience when you start making progress towards your goal. It makes you feel really fired up to keep going, and perhaps to try even harder because you know that your hard work is paying off.

2. If you measure your progress and find that you aren't on track, you can adjust your strategy and try to find a more successful one. It's far better to discover sooner rather than later what works and doesn't. The more you measure, the more you learn.

3. Many people love playing games. Setting challenging mini-goals and tracking your progress can psychologically turn what feels like work into a more exciting challenge, which you can even get quite addicted to. Suddenly, rather than dreading the weekly check-up on your progress, you can start to look forward to the opportunity to see just how far you have come.

What you should measure

Imagine that you were inspired by the story of Liz in the previous chapter and decided to try to lose 14 lbs through improving your fitness, attending your local gym. There are various different things that you could measure, for example:

- How much you weigh (compared with your target weight). This is important because this is your overall measure of success.

- How much weight you have lost each week. This is useful because it monitors progress towards your ultimate goal.

- The dimensions of your body, such as the size of your waist, hips and thighs. This can help because although your weight may not be going down, you may be building muscle, which means that your body shape is improving and you are becoming leaner.

- How much time you spend exercising each week, for example you might record that you did 45 minutes of exercise four times in one week.

This last measure is actually one of the most critical. It isn't directly measuring your actual target (i.e. weight) but it does measure activities which in theory should lead to you losing weight. This is called a **leading indicator**. A leading indicator is a step which, by doing, you would expect to move towards the achievement of a goal.

Leading indicators are great because they are within your control. It's difficult to control whether or not you lose a pound (an example of a **lagging indicator**, which only gives you feedback at the end of a specified period of time). However, it is far easier to control how many times a week you go to the gym and how long you exercise for.

Leading indicators are an effective tool because they help you to understand exactly what it is that actually makes the difference. The more you become aware of, and record, your activities, the greater your understanding of what leads to your ultimate measure of success.

For example, if you are weighing yourself weekly at the gym it can help to record what types of exercises you are doing and their intensity and duration, so over time, you can work out which of the exercises are having most impact. You might find that your time is better spent on the treadmill than spending the same period of time on an exercise bike. You can use these results to prioritize your time and activities to more effectively achieve weight loss.

Of course, it's still critical to measure your lagging indicators too. It's all very well keeping track of the effort you're putting in and having a nice little chart with boxes to colour in every time you do 30 minutes of exercise, and being proud of yourself when your chart is all coloured in. But if it doesn't actually make any difference to the overall lagging indicator then it is pointless.

With a goal of yours in mind, use this process to help you set your leading and lagging indicators:

- What is your overall measure of success? (e.g. to write a 40,000 word book)

- What is your target date for reaching that goal? (e.g. within two months)
- What do you need to achieve each day or week or each month to reach your overall target? (e.g. write about 5,000 words per week)
- Brainstorm all of the different ways that you can achieve your mini-goal (e.g. I can write for an hour every evening etc.)
- Look at the things you brainstormed. Which of the ideas you have come up with seems to be the most likely to enable you to reach your mini-goal? This is your 'goal-directed behaviour'.

The key to success is to measure your goal-directed behaviour (a leading indicator). If you have selected the right strategy, over time you will see progress towards your overall goal.

If you can't measure it you can't manage it

In 2008, a useful study was published in the American Journal of Preventative Medicine, based on findings by the Kaiser Permanente Center for Health Research. Researchers studied 1,685 overweight and obese adults and found that after five months, the average weight loss was 13 lbs per person.

Strikingly, the results showed that dieters who did not record what food they ate lost an average of 9 lbs, whereas people who kept a food diary for six days a week or more lost a staggering 18 lbs over the same period.

A food diary is useful because it helps you to spot patterns that lead to success and failure, which can help you to adjust your goal-directed behaviour. However, another key advantage of something like a weight-loss diary, where you record factors that impact on your goal achievement, is the psychological impact it can have on you.

Think about it – if you have to write down that you ate that extra doughnut at work today, it could make you think twice about eating it. There is a saying, 'What gets measured, gets done.' In this case, being measured can make you stop doing things that could make you fail – and start doing the things that make you succeed.

Don't just set indicators, set the *right* indicators

A salesperson's job and their pay may only be secured by the number of sales they make to clients. Some salespeople may use the power of numbers to help them in this, keeping tabs on the number of people in their Rolodex (or the modern day equivalent, their BlackBerry), how many meetings they have a week or how many phone calls they make.

All sound reasonable to you? They may well be using leading indicators (i.e the number of meetings they have a week) and they may look at their lagging indicators (i.e. the sales they've achieved), but are they using the right ones?

One salesperson who decided to use a different leading indicator was Joe Girard, a Chevrolet car salesman in Michigan. Joe's philosophy was, 'Your income in sales is directly related to your ability to nurture and build relationships.' So, to nurture relationships with his would-be customers he sent them personalized greeting cards.

He was sending over 14,000 cards out a month. His take on this was that 'Every one of those cards was worth its weight in gold.' Why? Because, through this behaviour, he was selling over 1,400 cars a year. That works out at nearly four cars sold by him every single day of the year, a stellar amount. In fact, Joe's approach was so successful at getting customers to come to him, that they were the ones who were making all the phone calls.

Joe's success was not in setting common leading indicators of how many calls he made, or how many meetings he arranged; it was through how many greeting cards were sent out. Joe was recognized by Guinness World Records as the world's greatest salesman thanks to him using a measurable approach he believed would work and provided good results when he tested it.

- If you have leading indicators in achieving your goal you'll be more likely and better able to accomplish it.
- If your leading activities don't match up with your lagging indicators, then change your activities.

- Record the efforts you're putting in and where you're putting them in, this will help you to assess whether they are the best ones to keep using.

 Create measurable steps that lead you towards your goal to help you to achieve overall success.

O: Opportunities

Seek and ye shall find.

Matthew 7:7

There's another reason why regularly monitoring your goals is useful. There is a benefit in keeping your goal at the forefront of your mind rather than in a forgotten-about diary at the back of a drawer.

Here's why. In 1999, researchers Chabris and Simons at Harvard University asked participants to watch a video of six people playing basketball. In the video, three of the players were dressed in white and three were dressed in black. Participants were asked to silently count the number of times the basketball was thrown between people in the team wearing the white shirts.

If you have ever seen this famous clip, you may well have come to the end of the video and answered, 'There were fifteen passes, that was pretty straightforward.'

But maybe it wasn't as straightforward as you would imagine.

Although it is almost impossible to believe, Chabris and Simons found that almost half of the participants watching the video failed to see a person dressed as a big hairy gorilla stroll right into the centre of the video, drum his chest and walk off again.

This research reveals that although we may be looking, we actually miss a lot of what goes on around us. Later in the chapter we'll tell you why spotting analogous gorillas is key to your success, but first try this experiment to explore the phenomenon of selective attention.

 It is very important that you do not cheat during this exercise; if you do you'll have missed a valuable experience that you'll only be able to have once in your life (but which you can then make all your friends do).

Find a pen and paper and draw two circles, like so:

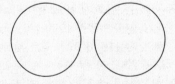

Within one circle, draw the head of a one pence coin (i.e. a low denomination coin from your currency) and in the other, draw the tail. Try to make the drawing as accurate as possible, without looking at the real coin.

When you have finished your drawing, compare it to the real coin. How accurately were you able to reproduce the penny? Now consider how often you touch a penny every week. Probably all the time, yet do you really know what one looks like?

Selective attention

If you didn't reproduce the head and tail of the penny very faithfully, you are certainly not alone. Having done this experiment with hundreds of people, we have seen a spectrum of results, many of them bad and none of them outstanding.

So why are we typically so bad at remembering the detail on a coin we use almost every day? Although we touch pennies all the time, many people are simply unable to recall the specifics of the pictures and writing upon them.

Unless there is a good reason, your brain will probably think that the detail on a penny is unimportant. The only things that you really need to know about a penny in everyday life are its size, shape, weight and colour. So even though it is possible that there could be a penny in your pocket or handbag right now, the powers of selective attention mean that you have always ignored the detail.

The reason we have this selective attention is that every second we are taking in an enormous amount of information through our five senses. For example, right now, can you:

- Taste anything in your mouth?
- Smell anything?
- Feel your legs against where you are sitting?
- Hear any faint background noises in the room you are in?
- See objects in the room in your peripheral vision?

You probably weren't aware of these things before your attention was directed towards them, but now we bet you can't help but notice them. Think of all of the information constantly bombarding your senses. There is far too much for us to be consciously aware of everything. Only a small amount of information makes it through the subconscious barrier. This is the information that our brain thinks is important.

Focusing attention through setting goals

So, how can selective attention be related to your success? Well, when you set a goal this tells your brain that information related to the achievement of this goal is important. The brain then knows to bring to your conscious attention anything relevant to that goal. Similarly, regular monitoring of your progress also constantly reminds you that paying conscious attention is still worthwhile.

But what is the impact?

Suddenly you start seeing opportunities to help you to achieve your goal, which were always there, but which you never paid attention to before. When you watch the gorilla video for a second time, your brain knows to look for the gorilla, as well as to count the passes, and you cannot fail to see it. You wonder how on earth you missed it in the first place.

One day, when I (Alison) was walking to the train station and contemplating our forthcoming wedding, I was somewhat obsessed with how sunny it was going to be, come the big day. On this particular occasion, I asked myself, 'I wonder what day of the year has the best weather to get married?'

I reached the train station, journeyed to London and walked to the Tube. As I sat on the platform, thinking about my upcoming meeting, something caught my attention. I could not believe my eyes. Right in front of me, in big bold print, were the words 'The UK's best day for weather is June 23rd'. Within hours, and without even trying, I had found out the answer to my question. The sentence was part of an advert for a national newspaper and was just one of a list of about ten facts, including the size of the world's largest hailstone.

What is significant here is that I didn't consciously notice any of the other facts on the list, or indeed any of the other adverts at the station. I just noticed that piece of information because it was relevant to what I'd been thinking.

Even more importantly, there are opportunities – big, hairy gorilla-sized opportunities – around us all the time – things that are interesting and relevant to us but that we don't see. That is, unless you have set a goal in place, bringing those things to your selective attention, in which case you *do* see the gorilla.

For example, let's say that you have set yourself the goal of learning to speak French. All of a sudden, you will start seeing things that can help you to learn French leaping out at you all the time. You flick through a newspaper and see an advert for French lessons. Your friend mentions that she has a French friend who has just arrived in your town. You are tuning the radio and you accidentally hit upon a French radio station. The point is that the world hasn't just magically started breeding opportunities to learn French – you just didn't notice them before because your brain wasn't noticing them for you.

One benefit of reviewing your progress towards your goals on a regular basis is that you will constantly be reminding your brain to keep searching for relevant information. In the midst of the hustle and bustle of life, your brain can have rather a lot to focus on, so give it a helping hand and keep gently reminding it that your goals are important to you.

TRY IT NOW!

Be warned, this exercise might start driving you nuts!

Pick something that you probably see in your environment but you don't normally consciously look for, for example a particular brand of car or pregnant ladies.

Tell your brain to start noticing the thing that you picked.

Before you know it, you will be completely surrounded by Ford Fiestas or baby bumps which were always there but which you never paid any attention to before.

You can use the power of selective attention to your advantage – tell a friend what your goal is and thereby activate their brain to look for opportunities to help you to achieve your goal too. Two brains with focused selective attention are, after all, better than one.

- Just because we're familiar with something doesn't mean we're always aware of it.
- Help get your brain into gear; become consciously aware of what it is you are looking for.
- Regular reviewing of goals helps to remind your brain to constantly look for the opportunities that are all around you that you might not otherwise see.

Just because we look, doesn't mean that we see – focus your attention through goal-setting and it will help you to spot new opportunities, which will then enable you to achieve those goals.

P: Preparation

Before anything else, preparation is the key to success.
Alexander Graham Bell

If you have ever attempted something particularly ambitious, such as starting your own business from scratch, you might have felt a tremendous pressure to be visibly successful really quickly.

Well meaning people ask, 'So how's it going?' and nobody wants to admit, 'Well I've been working day and night and so far I haven't even earned 10% of the money that I would have earned in my old job.' And it isn't only the pressure that we feel to prove ourselves to others. For our own self-esteem, we need to have proof that we made the right decision in taking action to achieve our dream and that the effort will be worth it.

If you aren't lucky enough to instantly make your dreams come true (and in all honesty that includes most of us!) it is worth noting a valuable lesson that nature can teach us about the importance of preparation. Introducing: the Chinese Bamboo tree.

When the seed of the Chinese Bamboo is planted, watered and fertilized there is no visible growth for four whole years. However, during the fifth year, it grows a staggering 90 feet (that's over 25 m) in just six weeks.

Did the tree really take all of that time to get ready to begin growing? Not at all. Although not visible, the root system experienced tremendous development during those first four years therefore making it possible for the rest of the plant to eventually grow tall and strong.

Reflect back on your life and think about a time when you felt stuck, as though you weren't making any progress, but then things clicked into place.

What seeds had you already sown that just needed time to grow?

What can you learn from this?

Success can sometimes happen when you least expect it. You can take decisive action but then get to a place where you feel stuck. Then, all of a sudden, an opportunity can present itself based on your efforts to date, and because of your groundwork, you are ready to grasp that opportunity.

We really want to give you a message of hope: action leaves a trail. If you've been working really hard to achieve your goal, but you still aren't seeing any tangible progress, it might feel like your efforts are fruitless. However, remember that your hard work will ultimately pay off. Even when times feel dark and you are feeling bewildered by your lack of progress, you are leaving behind a trail of work that is sowing the seeds of success. Given the right conditions, they will germinate.

All of a sudden the walls spring up

A dream that many people have is to build their own home. TV shows on the subject normally start with the diggers moving in to begin creating the foundations. The future residents of the home often comment on how slow the foundations are to complete and how frustrating it is to spend enormous amounts of money and see relatively little for it.

But these shows don't even show the half of it. People spend years getting ready to even begin the build, from deciding the location to build on to gaining planning consent, agreeing architect plans, researching building materials and finding reputable experts to help them.

Yet all of these steps are necessary in order to build the perfect house. Just like the Chinese Bamboo, it might take four years to get to the stage where the foundations are built but in the fifth year everything leaps up. The success is made by the preparation. After that initial planning period, the building springs out of the ground and the fruits of all that labour become far more visible.

The youngest Australian to conquer Everest

So just what preparation do you have to do to achieve success? Rex Pemberton is an inspirational person who can teach us all a thing or two about waiting to reach your goals. As Rex says:

There are no shortcuts to life's greatest achievements.

It took 21-year-old Rex just a single step to reach the summit of Mount Everest and watch his friend Ed scatter his dad's ashes on top of the world. However, the journey to the top began way before that.

Rex's dream to reach the summit of Everest began over a decade before, at the tender age of just 10. Here is just a flavour of what he had to do to be ready to achieve his dream:

Knowledge expansion: Rex needed to understand what permits were necessary to climb Everest and how weather patterns might impact upon his quest to reach the summit.

Logistical preparation: he needed to secure $100,000 in sponsorship, to fund travel, permits, Sherpa fees, equipment and food. He also had to gather all of the essential equipment for the trip and learn to use it safely.

Skill development: Rex gained experience of regular high terrain mountain climbs such as the Matterhorn and Mont Blanc, this included conquering steep terrain and sheer rock faces, and completing night climbs.

Physical preparation: he underwent intense physical training which included walking with a fully loaded backpack dragging a large rubber tyre through sand to build his strength and stamina.

Mental preparation: last but by no means least, he made mental preparations not only for the climb up, but also for the climb down, which is equally dangerous.

Rex's dream would have been impossible without all of this groundwork, which demonstrates the importance of all round preparation. If you haven't quite succeeded, it is worth checking that you aren't trying to run before you can walk.

 What do you need to do in order to prepare for success and achieve your dream? Have a think about this under the following headings:

- Knowledge expansion
- Logistical preparation
- Skill development
- Physical preparation
- Mental preparation.

As well as listing what you need to do to prepare under each heading, have a think about what resources or experiences are available that could help you.

The perils of not having all round preparation

It truly was a spine-tingling, hair-raising experience that followed after typing 'Susan Boyle' into YouTube and watching her unforgettable rendition of 'I Dreamed a Dream' from Les Misérables on Britain's Got Talent, the TV talent contest.

Susan Boyle's life was almost instantly transformed. Within a week she went from being an unassuming, Scottish spinster with a cat named Pebbles, to being an international star, largely due to her audition being viewed online more than 66 million times in that week, setting a new record.

However, very sadly, the day after coming second in the final of Britain's Got Talent, Susan Boyle had to be taken to the famous psychiatric clinic, The Priory. Susan had been completely unprepared for the enormous attention she received, and the intense media focus on her.

Susan had put down some very firm roots in developing her singing skills. She had received vocal coaching, attended the Edinburgh Acting School and had even recorded a charity album, creating 1,000 copies. However, despite having the most incredible singing voice, performing at the Edinburgh Fringe festival and singing in pubs and churches, she was not prepared mentally for becoming such a sensation.

Thankfully, Susan Boyle was strong enough to recover and went on to record her first album, which became a number one bestseller on music charts around the world. She has since been recognized by Guinness World Records for having the fastest selling debut album by a female artist in the UK, the most successful first week of sales for a debut album in the UK, and has also been awarded the record for being the oldest person to reach number one with a debut album in the UK.

- The fruits of your efforts may not be immediately clear, but if you keep on nurturing your dream it can blossom.
- Lasting success rarely happens overnight, instead there may be a process of putting effort into something for years before it finally takes off.
- There are many ways to prepare for success, and the better you are able to have all round preparation, the better your chances of success become.

 The foundation of success is the preparation you put in place.

Q: Quick wins

Win small, win early, win often.

Gary Hamel

If you are finding that you are getting frustrated with how long it is taking you to achieve your goal, and want some help staying motivated, you need to understand the enormous power of a tiny little molecule in your brain called dopamine. So, what is dopamine? The experience of being a goldfish owner can be quite revealing.

We have two pet goldfish in our household. Quite surprisingly, given the death rate of plants that enter our house, our fish have now made it to the grand old age of 3½ years. This is particularly surprising given how much we hated cleaning out their tank.

Anyone who has had a goldfish will know that they can grow quite large quite quickly. So big, in fact, that we found the fish were beginning to outgrow their home. Therefore, one day last year, we embarked upon the task of trying to purchase a new tank. Little did we realize just how much choice there is out there.

And this is where dopamine kicks in. As you scan the internet and pet stores looking at all of the different options, your brain is constantly giving little dopamine surges every time you see a product. Some dopamine surges are bigger than others. This is because the level of dopamine is designed to signal how much 'expected pleasure' each option will give you. The more expected pleasure, the bigger the dopamine surge. And when you see something that really fits the bill, you get a massive dopamine hit.

And boy did it hit! We came across a fish tank called the BiOrb Life, and boom – we really wanted it. Apart from the potential to look amazing in our kitchen (it has some rather funky blue mood lighting) the major benefit of this particular fish tank was the fact that it was almost entirely self-cleaning. Happy days for the fish and the owners.

So, dopamine helped us to make our choice. But that's not the end of the story.

You can probably identify with the feeling of deciding you want something and then wanting it *really* badly. You can't stop thinking about it, everything you do reminds you of it, and you can't rest until you have it. Bizarrely (and as much as we hate to admit it) this was how we began to feel about having a BiOrb Life tank. The thought of never cleaning out fish poo ever again had given us a massive surge in dopamine and now this powerful chemical was continuing to fire and keep us focused on the thought of buying that tank.

And do not underestimate the power of dopamine once it hits. For anyone who has been to Las Vegas and on your way to breakfast, seen people still sitting at the same slot machine as when you walked past them to go to dinner the night before – that is dopamine at work. When you get a large payout from a slot machine, you receive an enormous surge of dopamine. Once your brain has realized that you can receive pleasure from this activity, dopamine keeps you well and truly focused on putting more money into the slots, trying to work out how you can get an even bigger payoff. Sadly the house always wins!

After just four days, we caved in and bought that fish tank (despite it being way over budget) and the pleasure we got from opening the box was worth it. So, dopamine gave its third and final kick – the moment of satisfaction when you actually achieve your goal.

THINK ABOUT IT

Think of a time when you scanned a range of possible products to buy and got a massive dopamine hit – that feeling of, 'I must have this!' How did that feeling of longing drive you to behave and how did you feel when you eventually got your product?

When the dopamine stops firing

One of the most interesting roles of dopamine is the part that it plays in hedonic adaptation, which we discussed back in Chapter B.

On unpacking our new fish tank we experienced a surge of pleasure and excitement. But a curious aspect of dopamine is that once you have achieved your goal, if your brain can't see any future benefit in continuing to pursue it (i.e. it is a one-off benefit) the dopamine ceases to fire. This very powerful molecule has done its job of driving you to get something that would bring you benefit. It stops firing because your brain recognizes that it has accomplished its mission.

Again, it's not something that we like to admit to, but the action of dopamine ceasing to fire is why after just a few days of buying our new tank, we thought 'How about a new picture on the wall to complement the new tank? That would be nice.' So, we jumped on the internet and the whole cycle started again.

THINK ABOUT IT

Can you think of a time when you decided that you wanted something *really* badly, but you couldn't get it for some reason and after a while, you just stopped wanting it?

Dopamine-fired goal achieving

So why did you stop wanting something that you previously wanted really badly? Your brain gives you a dopamine hit when it senses expected pleasure. But when an item is out of reach, your brain stops signalling expected pleasure because its achievement doesn't seem possible. You begin to lose your attention and start to focus somewhere else.

So, in summary, dopamine is relevant to goal-setting because:

- When you have that powerful feeling of wanting to achieve a goal, dopamine is at work.
- The more you feel that you want to achieve your goal, the more powerful the dopamine hit and the better it will focus your attention on achieving it.
- Just like gambling, dopamine will make you addicted to trying to get the reward from achieving your goal.

Creating dopamine hits through seeking quick wins

Anyone who has been to a penny arcade will know just how much excitement you can get from an afternoon spending as little as, say, £4.72. That's at least 472 shots at making the coins fall off the shelf. It doesn't really matter that you only won 32p – that chink, chink, chink noise just feels so great and keeps you there for hours.

Perhaps even more curiously, if you are an iPhone user you may have experienced the phenomenon of having your life taken over for a few days because you are completely obsessed with playing a game that you downloaded from the App Store.

There is a game called *Coin Push Frenzy* which is a virtual penny arcade, and it is every bit as addictive when you are playing for the pointless reward of opening virtual gift boxes as when you are playing for real money.

So, it doesn't actually matter what the size of the reward is. What is important is your brain's estimation of how much pleasure you will get from the reward – and clearly the thought of opening a virtual box is enough of a reward for us humans (indeed, dopamine is the foundation of the video game industry just as it is of the casino industry).

As long as you get a win, even a small one, and as long as you think that if you keep going you will get more wins, this will motivate you to keep trying.

By breaking a goal down into a series of steps, like you learned in Chapter 1, you create the opportunity to experience quick wins. Your brain will realize that this mini-goal *is* achievable and sets about predicting the expected pleasure from you achieving the next mini-goal.

As a result of your brain giving you the thumbs-up, you focus your day-to-day actions to achieve the mini-goal. And, unlike the fish tank ceasing to be motivating because it was a one-off goal, your dopamine doesn't stop firing after you've achieved the first mini-goal. This is because you can get a 'pay-off' from aiming for the next target.

Keep winning and you'll keep going

A final lesson that we can learn from slot machines concerns the payout percentage. Slot machines are typically programmed to pay out 82–98% of the money put in. Why so high? Clearly it can't be more than 100% (otherwise the casinos wouldn't make any money) but the payout needs to be high enough that it keeps us coming back for more, hoping for that bumper payout that will leave us 'up' in our winnings. If the payout ratio was only 10% we would quickly lose interest because our dopamine levels would tell us that this doesn't bring enough benefit.

So when it comes to goal-setting, and setting sub-goals, whilst we advocate aiming for the moon with your overall goal, you will be far more likely to succeed if you break your goal down into easy to achieve but pleasurable sub-goals and get addicted to achieving them. If you are finding that you are suffering from demotivation, it might well be worth breaking your sub-goals down further so that you are able to 'win' more frequently and stay motivated to succeed.

Review your overall target and the sub-goals that you have set.

Ask yourself, 'Will I get pleasure from achieving these and are they easily achievable?'

If each sub-goal is taking a while to achieve then it might be worth breaking them down further, to give yourself new milestones.

If achieving the sub-goals isn't particularly pleasurable in its own right, perhaps think of giving yourself some rewards when you reach milestones towards your goal. Alternatively, do something as simple as creating a chart where you colour in the squares as you reach each milestone. Such a simple technique can be surprisingly motivating.

- You will keep motivated by experiencing rewards along the path to your goal.
- Break your goal down into sub-goals, so that you can more easily achieve these and experience the pleasure from completing them.
- If your sub-goals aren't pleasurable enough, add some extra rewards in.

You're going to be more likely to achieve your goals if you receive a regular surge of dopamine from having a series of quick wins.

R: Rosenthal effect

If you want to fly with the eagles you can't continue to scratch with the turkeys.

Zig Ziglar

If, despite all the action you have taken so far, you are still finding it hard to succeed, it might well be worth considering the impact that others are having upon you.

In 1968 Robert Rosenthal and Lenore Jacobson administered an intelligence test on a class of primary school children at 'Oak School' (a pseudonym) in San Francisco. The teachers were told that the purpose of the intelligence test was twofold. Firstly, it would measure the IQ of the children and secondly it would predict the 20% of students who, regardless of their performance to date, would be likely to make the most progress during the forthcoming academic year. The teachers were then told who the predicted top improvers or 'bloomers' would be.

At the end of the academic year, eight months later, the intelligence test was repeated again and, perhaps not surprisingly, the results showed that the 20% of children who had been predicted to improve the most, did in fact do so. They showed, on average, an increase of 12 IQ points on the test, compared with an increase of only 8 points for the other children. The increase was even larger for the 'bloomers' in younger classes, who showed, on average a 20-point increase on the test.

But the twist in the story is that no results of any test were used to predict who would be the top performers. Instead, the lucky children who the teachers were told would be the 'bloomers' were randomly selected and given this label as a matter of chance.

This study shows that the label that you are given, and your interaction with others who are aware of that label, can have a significant impact on the results that you achieve. Frighteningly, this occurs even when you do not know that you have even been given that label. This phenomenon has been called the **Rosenthal Effect**. It is also known as the **Pygmalion Effect**, linked most famously to the George Bernard Shaw play Pygmalion, which shows the impact that two men have in the transformation of a bedraggled flower girl into a well-spoken lady.

For ethical reasons the researchers at 'Oak School' only concentrated on trying to produce positive results in the children's performance. However, it is worth asking yourself what the results of also identifying the 20% of students who were least likely to improve in the following academic year might have been. A scary thought.

So how do the negative reactions of others hold us back? We can learn a valuable lesson from a fable about frogs…

One day, a bunch of tiny frogs decided to run (or hop!) a race. The aim of the race was to be the first frog to reach the top of a very tall tower.

A large group of spectators gathered to watch the event. Even before the race had started, they began saying to themselves, 'How will they ever reach the top? It's too difficult.'

The race began and the eager frogs embarked upon climbing the tower. One by one, the exhausted contestants began to drop out.

The crowd were yelling, 'You haven't got a hope, you'll never make it!' The last few frogs in the race kept going, much to the crowd's disbelief. 'It's impossible, you'll never get to the top!'

Finally, all but one frog had given up, and with triumph, he reached the top. The astonished crowd, rushed to the frog and in their jubilations they wanted to know how on earth he did it.

It turned out the winning frog was deaf.

THINK ABOUT IT Think of an occasion when someone you know has believed in your potential and encouraged you and this helped you to succeed.

Think of an occasion when someone that you know undermined your confidence in your ability to achieve something and this held you back.

Social influences upon success

A former Professor in Psychology, Dr David McClelland was very interested in the question of whether there was any correlation between the people you associate with and the results that you get in life.

After 25 years of research on the topic of achievement he concluded that the choice of a negative 'reference group' was in itself enough to condemn a person to failure and underachievement in life. Your reference group is the people you work with, live with and spend time with. And their attitudes and opinions rub off on you.

The choices you make about the friends and associates who you have relationships with have a big impact on your future. So choose the people you spend time with carefully. Over time this 'reference group' will influence you because they are having an effect on your thinking, your personality, your health and on every event that happens to you. Make sure that influence is the best it can be.

Keep away from people who try to belittle your ambitions. Small people always do that, but the really great ones make you feel that you, too, can become great.

Mark Twain

A success safety net

In 1973 the publishing company Doubleday accepted a book script about a teenage girl called Carietta White. The book, entitled *Carrie*, was submitted by an aspiring writer called Stephen King, the very same Stephen King who has now successfully sold over 350 million books, with a number of them made into movies.

However, not everybody knows that Stephen's story could have been very different. When he initially started working on Carrie he was frustrated with the story to the point where he threw his manuscript into the rubbish bin.

Thankfully for Stephen, and his now legions of fans, somebody else was with him on his journey who refused to believe he wasn't good enough. His wife, Tabitha, reclaimed the manuscript from the rubbish, read it through and, impressed by it, encouraged Stephen to carry on. He did, and after the book was accepted by Doubleday a deal was signed worth $400,000. Not bad for something Stephen had become convinced was junk.

There are people in life that will naturally support and encourage you. There are others who will tell you that you are mad for even trying and that what you are aiming for is impossible. These people's own life circumstances, attitudes and failures will ultimately have an impact on you.

Associations are both subtle and powerful.
Jim Rohn

TRY IT NOW!

Undertake an 'associations audit'.

1. Think of the five people who are most influential in your life.

2. Draw a grid and write each person's initials in a column heading.

3. Give a grade answer between A–F to each question shown in our example grid below. A is the best possible score, F is the worst possible score.

Question	Mark	Sarah	Peter	Jo	Suzy
How positive is this person about their own life?	A	C	F	B	E
How much success has this person experienced themselves?	B	C	E	A	F
How much does this person genuinely believe in my ability to succeed?	A	B	D	B	A
How much does this person genuinely want me to succeed?	A	E	C	A	D

Choosing your associations wisely

Looking at the exercise you have done, let's now interpret the results. Keep in mind the rankings you've given to your associations based on their abilities and successes, and their thoughts about yours.

For those people who you have generally graded positively (A–B):
- Aim to spend the most time with these people
- Discuss your goals, dreams and ambitions with them
- Ask them for input on how you could achieve your goals and their assistance as you seek to do so.

For those people who you have graded as average (C–D):
- Limit your discussions with them about your ambitions
- Limit the time you spend with them when you are in the process of pursuing a goal, they could unintentionally cause the wind to come out of your sails.

For those people who you have graded negatively (E–F):
- Don't discuss your ambitions openly with them as they may attempt to find fault with them
- Potentially distance yourself from them, though this may not be easy to do, especially if they are family
- Refrain from involving them in your goal-setting and goal achievements.

Positive beliefs about ourselves and others are fragile things that should be nurtured, not trampled over. Because there can be so many people giving you their unsolicited views about what you should, or should not, be aiming for, and how you should go about achieving those things, the next chapter will explore what to do if someone gives you a negative label – and how to overcome this.

In the meantime, remember that if possible it is best to avoid sharing your vision and dreams too closely with 'mood hoovers' because if you aren't careful, however well meaning they may be, they could influence you to fail when you are in fact capable of succeeding.

- Ask yourself, 'Who am I surrounding myself with on a regular basis and what impact are they having upon me?'
- Learn to spot those who are supporting you and those who are holding you back – spend more time with the former and less with the latter.
- Take action to prevent negative people from dragging you down and stopping you reaching your goals.

 The Rosenthal Effect shows that your success levels can be influenced by your associations with others, so make sure that they're the best so that you can become your best.

S: Self-belief

It is easier to avoid the effects of others' negativity when we question if an action or attitude is appropriately directed at us. If it isn't, we can choose to sidestep it and let it pass.

Sue Patton Theole

You may well have faced a moment in life where *you* know what you are capable of doing, but your parents – who almost certainly only want the best for you – have other ideas as to the right way forward.

A lady called Joanne faced just this situation. She was convinced that the only thing that she wanted from life was to be a writer. In contrast, her parents felt that being a writer was an unsuitable and frankly amusing career choice. They clearly believed, and explicitly told Joanne, that a career as a writer would *never* fund either a mortgage or a worthwhile pension. Having come from impoverished backgrounds, Joanne's parents simply wanted more for their daughter than they had had themselves.

In Joanne's life, over the next ten years, things got considerably worse. Her mother died and her marriage was a complete disaster, lasting just two years. She walked out of her marriage and into poverty, carrying a tiny baby and suffering from clinical depression.

In her own words, Joanne said that, 'The fears that my parents had for me, and that I had for myself, had both come to pass and by every useful standard, I was the biggest failure I knew.'

In the previous chapter, we talked about the impact of the beliefs of those around you and how much they can influence what you achieve. With Joanne's parents having told her that she should give up on her 'pie in the sky' idea of being a writer, and with literary experts and publishing houses rejecting her book idea on numerous occasions saying that it 'wasn't very commercial', you can absolutely understand why Joanne might have given up. Her parents' prophecy, that you cannot earn a living through being a writer, could absolutely have come true for her.

So our question to you is this: when you have been told that you will fail and that circumstance has indeed come true, is it possible to break a negative self-fulfilling prophecy and get the results you so desperately want?

 Can you think of any examples of when you (or someone else) were able to break a negative self-fulfilling prophecy? How did this happen?

Choosing a better prophecy

In Chapter D, we introduced the concept of a self-fulfilling prophecy which was a phrase coined by Robert Merton. As well as introducing the concept, Robert Merton explained the specific circumstances in which it can also be broken.

He explained that there are two important conditions that enable a negative self-fulfilling prophecy to be broken:

1. The assumption on which the self-fulfilling prophecy is based is questioned.
2. The person affected rejects the fear associated with the self-fulfilling prophecy coming true.

Let's take a look at each of those in turn.

Questioning the assumption that the prophecy is based on

In the example our struggling writer, Joanne, was told that she could not earn an acceptable living through being a writer. What is key here is that this is not an absolute fact, it is just a belief. Although many people struggle to earn a living through writing, others are capable of achieving this.

Take the example of Stephen King from the previous chapter. Stephen was paid an advance of $2,000 to write a book that he would have to spend months working on, with no promise of any future earnings if nobody bought any of the books.

When the book was eventually completed (thanks to his wife fishing it out of the bin) the publisher sold on the rights to another publisher. Stephen King was entitled to half of the proceeds, pocketing $200,000 from the deal (worth about $1million in today's money), which allowed him to quit his teaching job and take up writing full-time.

So it is *not* true that people cannot earn a living from writing books. Stephen King has since gone on to land some significant book deals, with earnings estimated at over $80 million in the process.

Rejecting the fear associated with the prophecy coming true

People who are able to break the self-fulfilling prophecy also have to accept that the negative consequences associated with the prophecy coming to fruition may actually occur, but they are courageous enough to proceed in any case.

Such a decision should not be taken lightly. You should always think about the consequences of your decisions and should not take reckless risks. However, successful people consistently show that they are prepared to acknowledge their fear and go ahead none the less. It is also interesting to stop and reflect upon the advice we heard from our wise elders back in Chapter A – with hindsight, they wished they had taken more risks in life.

Breaking the prophecy

So how did things turn out for our aspiring writer, Joanne?

Well, you know the outcome already. If you haven't guessed by now, Joanne, 'Jo', is better known to all of us as J. K. Rowling. She has inspirationally proved to us that it is possible, although immensely challenging, to break a self-fulfilling prophecy.

Even when the first three chapters of the manuscript for her first book, Harry Potter and the Philosopher's Stone, were finally accepted by a small publisher in London, Jo was still told by her editor that she should probably consider getting a second job because she had little chance of making money in children's books.

But boy, did she prove everyone wrong. By 2010 J. K. Rowling was estimated to be the twelfth richest woman in Great Britain, with Forbes giving her an estimated net worth of $1 billion. The final instalment of her series, Harry Potter and the Deathly Hallows, was the fastest selling book of all time and she is credited for doing more for literacy than any other person alive.

You see, what has made J.K. Rowling successful is that she did not accept the assumption that you cannot earn a living from writing.

In her interview with Oprah Winfrey, J.K. Rowling describes what she calls an almost 'clairvoyant-type' moment. One day, having been working on the first Harry Potter book in a café, as she walked home she said to herself that the hardest thing would be for her to get published. If she could just do that, it would be huge. She believed that if she could overcome the hurdle of getting noticed, then she could fulfil her dreams of writing for a living (although she didn't foresee quite how much it would make her!). After all, since the age of five or six it was the only thing she had ever wanted to do in life. Despite the odds being against her, she never let go of her self-belief that she could earn a living from being a writer.

Later in the Oprah interview, J.K. Rowling gave us these words of wisdom:

> You've got to believe. I was not the world's most secure person. I'd say I was someone with not much self-belief at all. Yet in this one thing in my life I believed. I believed that I could tell a story.

J.K. Rowling was extremely brave. Whilst many would call her stupid for even contemplating being a writer whilst living literally hand-to-mouth with a baby to feed, Jo stayed resolute.

This admittedly was made easier by the fact that because she had nothing, she also had nothing to lose. But Jo also made a conscious choice *not* to go and get a job teaching, which would have brought in a modest income. Instead she pursued her dream with complete belief.

Perhaps one of the most difficult things to overcome in this situation is the fear of what other people think of you. Whether you like it or not, society does judge you and label you. One person's heroine is another person's welfare-dependent, irresponsible single mother!

Through her success, J.K. Rowling is now in a position to provide her child with more of a future than virtually any other parent in the UK. Also, unlike many people who have become rich and who take their earnings offshore, J.K. Rowling remains a full UK taxpayer and contributes much more to the country than she ever received in welfare.

Think about the goal that you have set yourself.

- What negative comments do you think others would make about your goal/vision?
- How can you challenge the assumption that their belief is right? After all, a belief is in their heads and is not fundamentally real.

- We don't have to accept another person's label of us.
- Question the basis people have for their advice, finding evidence to the contrary.
- Don't accept the fear and negativity, focus instead on the possibility.

A final magical twist in J.K. Rowling's fascinating story can be found by looking on page fifteen of Harry Potter and the Philosopher's Stone. As Professor Dumbledore and Professor McGonagall are leaving Harry on the doorstep of his aunt and uncle's house, McGonagall says, 'He'll be famous ... every child in our world will know his name.'

Now that's a positive self-fulfilling prophecy if ever we saw one!

 Have self-belief and overcome the negative labels and opinions of others – their prophecies are often unfounded and we can best overcome them by proving them wrong.

T: Team

There is no such thing as a self-made man. You will reach your goals only with the help of others.

George Shinn

In the last couple of chapters we've explored how other people can hold you back. Now's the time to look at the other side of the coin and examine how other people *can* help you to succeed.

Imagine standing in front of thousands of people in a theatre in Hollywood, with many millions watching you on TV, as you receive an Oscar. On the face of it, you have just been credited with the top prize for your work. Well done you.

Except, when you deliver the acceptance speech, you thank the many, many people who have supported you, mentored you, coached you and challenged you to develop yourself to get to this point. Your success is as much theirs as it is yours, and no one will be more proud of you than this team you have around you.

Whenever you see Padraig Harrington, the 2007–08 British Open golfing and 2008 US PGA Championship winner, or any golfer for that matter, walking around the course it seems a pretty lonely time. It's just them and their caddy for company. What you haven't seen is the hours of assistance that this person has received.

When Padraig is competing, it's not just him out there. In fact, he has a core team of seven people supporting him: a coach, a sports psychologist, a sports scientist, a physiotherapist, a marketing and PR agent, a fitness consultant, and of course, his caddy. Each member of this core team has their own special role in making Padraig perform at the top of his game.

When Ellen MacArthur became the fastest person to sail solo, non-stop, around the world in just over 71 days, she certainly didn't do it alone. After she had broken the record in 2005 she paid tribute to the onshore team who had supported her around the clock. Ellen told the BBC:

> A record is nothing if not shared. I'm proud of the record but I'm even more proud to be working with the best team in the world. When I was out there I was never ever alone, there was always a team of people behind me, in mind if not in body.

It wasn't just the support that she received from this team that contributed to her success. There was another critical player and a team behind that. Its name was Moby, and it was the boat that she made the voyage in.

> She's a fighter, a boat that will not let you down ... the team who built her are responsible for the fact that I am here, right now, safe and well and also with a record.

Without the team who built Moby and supported Ellen around the clock, she wouldn't have achieved the world record.

> *The ascent of Everest was not the work of one day,*
> *nor even of those few anxious, unforgettable weeks in*
> *which we prepared and climbed … It is, in fact, a tale of*
> *sustained and tenacious endeavour by many,*
> *over a long period of time.*
>
> Sir John Hunt

Our view of other's success is often that it has been a lonely pursuit, like Ellen and Padraig. They are, after all, the ones who turned up, put in the effort, and are receiving the rewards. But in truth, once a person has set a goal or target, their peers, friends, families and other important figures lend themselves to a 'success team' that help them on their way to that goal.

 Look back at the achievements you have made in your life so far. Consider your relationships with your friends, family and loved ones, consider your career, home, finances and leisure activities.

Take some time to write an acceptance speech to the people who have helped you to make these achievements possible: for example, the teachers who gave you far more than just academic knowledge. Thank them for what they have done for you, specifically saying how they have helped you and how much their support has meant to you.

If you are feeling really brave, share the relevant parts of your acceptance speech with the people you are thanking. Your recognition and appreciation will mean the world to them.

Your support circle

In a study by Norcross and Vangarelli into New Year's resolutions they followed 200 people over two years to monitor how they got on with keeping their resolutions.

77% maintained their pledges for one week but only 19% made them stick for two years. One of the biggest findings was that the more time that went by, the more important social support was for the participants to carry on with their resolution.

Another study, by Wing and Jeffrey, followed a group who were on a four-month weight loss program. Members were split into those who were on their own, and those who were there with a small circle of friends.

Six months after the weight loss program finished the results were examined. 76% of those who went on the program alone had completed it, and 24% had maintained their weight loss. In comparison, a staggering 95% of the group that had received social support had completed the program and 66% of these participants maintained their weight loss. This group also reported that they had lost more weight and been successful in keeping more of it off.

So whatever it is you are seeking to achieve in life, the research points to the fact that you will be more likely to achieve it if you take others along for company, or have them as your support team.

Get a-head (or a few)

When it comes to social support there are a wide number of options available to you.

Your friends, family, colleagues and acquaintances are the most obvious source of support. They are readily available (mostly) and will probably have helped you or been helped by you before. The downside to this group is that they may not be specialists in what you're trying to achieve, and they can be less objective in their opinions. If they are unlikely to appreciate your goal, or if they consider it unrealistic, they may unintentionally hold you back (if this is the case, buy them their own copy of this book so that you can support each other!).

An alternative is to consider somebody who you are not immediately familiar with who can provide an objective input, or who can act as an advisor or a mentor.

When Les Brown was an aspiring motivational speaker in the 1980s he forwarded an audio cassette of his keynote speech to Dr Norman Vincent Peale, a champion of positive thinking. When Peale heard it and spotted the potential in it he took Les under his wing. Peale committed to improving Les's style, developing him and opening doors for him to get better, higher paying speaking engagements. That was the power of a mentoring relationship to Les – it opened up opportunities for him to achieve his career aspirations as the motivational speaker we see today. Without that relationship he might never have achieved his goal.

Another option to get the support you need is through something called a mastermind group. Popularized by Napoleon Hill in his 1937 book *Think and Grow Rich*, a mastermind group is a small group of diverse experts who aren't in competition with each other and who are prepared to help each other. Henry Ford, the pioneer behind Ford cars, had a mastermind group that included the likes of Thomas Edison. Ford and Edison, two of the greatest men of that era, made a powerful combination. Bill Gates is also said to have benefited from having a mastermind group (and look where he got to).

Consider the goal that you have set yourself.

- Who within your immediate network can provide the assistance you need in the pursuit of your goal?
- If there is not someone within your network who can provide you with objective support, would an external specialist like a life coach be beneficial? They may be able to help challenge you and work through options.
- If you need somebody with direct experience of what it is you are trying to achieve, who could be a suitable mentor for you? Draw up a list of potential candidates.

If you have a particularly complex, long-term goal that needs a diverse range of expertise, consider setting up or joining a mastermind group. If setting one up, identify the specialists you would like to hold council with and identify what you have to offer them in return.

In gaining social support for what you are looking to achieve the most important step is the first one. So go ahead, take action and ask the people you have identified above for their support. We're sure they'll be flattered to be asked, and if they can they may well say yes.

- Success may often appear an individual pursuit, but in truth there is a support network behind every individual.
- Whatever goal you have set yourself, try to take somebody on the journey with you who has an interest in you achieving your goal and who will support you.
- Your current networks, coaches, mentors or other dedicated groups can provide you with the support that will sustain you in the pursuit of your goal.

 You will be better able to maintain pursuit of your goal, and eventually achieve it, through a network of support – your 'success team'.

U: Under pressure

A lot of directors don't want the pressure of a movie the size of Pearl Harbor. But I love it. I thrive on it.

Michael Bay

It is 1917 and your name is Katherine Briggs. You are 42 years old and live in Washington D.C. It is Christmas time and your daughter Isabel, who is 20, has brought home a young gentleman called Clarence whom you are meeting for the first time. How do you think you would react?

Like any parent, you would examine him with a keen eye! When Katherine did this, she found that Clarence was an admirable young man but at the same time, his personality was 'different' to other members of the family. He was so different, in fact, that she began researching the nature of personality.

Isabel actually describes the meeting of Clarence and her mother as a massive stroke of luck, because it led to the birth of the 'Myers-Briggs' typology of personality.

The Myers-Briggs Type Indicator (or MBTI for short) is a world famous personality test and well worth taking if you have never done it. One of the most interesting things that it looks at is your attitude to stress and pressure and the impact that they have upon your performance.

There are four scales on the MBTI test, one of which is called the J-P scale. This scale is the one that is relevant to dealing with stress and pressure, so we will tell you a little more about it now. If you want to find out more about the other scales there is lots of information on the internet – just type MBTI into a search engine.

The J-P scale of the MBTI classifies people into two key groups: J for Judging and P for Perceiving (don't worry about the psychobabble scale names themselves).

People with a J preference typically live by the ethos 'work first, play later'. They enjoy planning things and when they have a goal, they make slow and steady progress towards that goal. They tend to make decisions sooner rather than later, as this enables them to make progress more quickly. Last minute changes frustrate them because they can undo all of the hard work that they have already done.

In contrast, those with a P preference typically live by the ethos 'take action when you can't put it off any longer'. They don't like to make decisions until they have to be made, as they like keeping their options open. Last minute changes don't worry them too much because they do much of the work at the last minute anyway. When they have a goal, they know when the deadline is, but most of the work to meet the deadline is done close to it, when the pressure is on.

 Imagine that you are about to embark upon a trip to cross North America. What would you do before you leave for that trip? Find a pen and paper and make a list.

Having done this exercise with hundreds of people who have taken the MBTI test, it is fascinating to see the results. Those with a J preference typically write a massive list of things to do, whilst the Ps say, 'find my passport, book a ticket, bring my credit card and toothbrush and read the guidebook on the plane'! Which was your approach more like?

The exercise that you did obviously isn't a hard and fast test of what preference you have, you would need to take the real MBTI test to get an accurate picture. However, from this exercise, and from the descriptions above, you will probably already have gained an idea of which camp you fall into.

Personality and pressure

So how is this J and P stuff relevant to pressure? One of the key differences between people with a J preference and people with a P preference is the impact that last minute pressure has on them.

People with a J preference tend to get stressed by last minute pressure and this can impair their performance, as they can begin to panic. In contrast, people with a P preference tend to be energized by last minute pressure. It gives them the kick that they need to put in the hard work.

You can see this difference, for example, in university students. Some will prefer to get their essays done and out of the way and then go down to the pub. Others will live by partying first and then pulling an all-nighter to get the essay done when they absolutely have to.

What is important is that usually both groups of students will make the deadline and can get similar marks. However, the timeline in which they work towards their goal does differ. And critically, if they are forced to meet their goal in a way that does not align to their preferences this can be very frustrating and stressful, perhaps leading to worse results overall.

So what do I need to do when approaching my goal?

Some people might automatically think that pressure is bad, but there is actually a difference between stress and pressure. Stress is when pressure causes a negative emotion. However, for some, pressure is energizing.

It is well worth trying to analyze the impact that pressure has on you. Think of yourself like a battery – does pressure drain your battery or does it energize it? This is part of a larger ethos that we have in life, which is about understanding more generally what (or even who) drains your battery and what (or who) energizes it.

As with all aspects of your personality, you should play to your strengths. If you find that last minute pressure is energizing, don't be afraid to ignore the advice of others who say you are being foolish for leaving things too late. Just be very aware of your own capabilities and boundaries and try and work out how much pressure gives you the optimum results.

In contrast, if you are someone who hates last minute pressure, planning will be really important and useful to you, including building in contingency time to avoid situations where you feel stressed. Plus, for those with a J preference, it is also worth planning in 'down time' and sticking to it, as there can be a tendency to be a bit of a workaholic, trying to get things done even when you are resting.

If you are trying to achieve a goal that requires input from other people it is well worth trying to understand their preferences as well. For example, if you have a J preference and are waiting upon information or a decision from someone with a P preference, this can drive you nuts. If you have a P preference then working with someone who wants to make progress and decisions before you are ready to can be equally frustrating. Understanding your needs (and the needs of others) and articulating them can benefit relationships and help you make progress.

When the pressure is happening, right now!
So far, this chapter has looked at our reaction to stress and pressure when approaching something that might take anywhere from a few hours, to a couple of years to complete. But how do you cope when the pressure is occurring

right now? Why is it that some people crack under that immediate, intense pressure, and others thrive?

Take, for example, two national football teams competing against each other in the quarter-finals of the World Cup, facing the prospect of a penalty shoot out. It is likely that both teams feel butterflies in their stomachs and their hearts beat a little more quickly. Their bodies are preparing themselves with the 'fight or flight' response.

What is critical in this instant before kicking the ball from the penalty spot is how you psychologically interpret those bodily signals. As we said earlier in the book, 'Nothing has meaning except for the meaning we give to it ourselves.'

If you are a football fan you may be interested to hear that the word 'anxiety' is derived from the Latin word *angere* which means 'to choke' (this helps to explain the commonly used phrase of 'choking under pressure').

Some people psychologically interpret these bodily feelings as fear. As an England footballer lines up to take a penalty, he is likely to start seeing images in his mind of damning newspaper headlines the next day if he fails. After all, England has now lost penalty shoot-outs in five major tournaments.

In contrast Germany has not lost a penalty shoot-out since 1976. A German footballer may therefore interpret the exact same feelings differently – the adrenaline flowing is getting them pumped up to succeed at the challenge before them.

So even though our bodies respond the same when under pressure, the way that our brains interpret these signals can be different.

How to perform under pressure

Here are some tips to help you learn how you can perform better under pressure:

1. **Learn to interpret your bodily signals differently.** A useful technique for this is the ABC technique, which you learnt in Chapter F, and which looks at your beliefs and the consequences that are caused by an event.

2. **Use a pre-performance routine.** This means that you force yourself to focus on carrying out a set pattern of activities, all within your control, stopping you from focusing on any negative thinking.

3. **Use positive self-talk.** Be aware of the little voice in your head. If it is saying, 'The newspapers are going to cremate me tomorrow.' this will have very different effects upon your anxiety levels than saying, 'I'm going to kick this ball accurately and it's going to land exactly where I want it to.'

4. **Visualize yourself succeeding.** Just as the tip above focuses on what you say to yourself, this focuses on the pictures you see in your mind's eye. Visualizing success is covered in more detail in the next chapter.

5. **Get a decent amount of sleep.** When we are under pressure, there is often a tendency to turn into a workaholic and burn the midnight oil. However, research shows how important being well rested is to our performance. For example, when revising for a critical exam, sleep is necessary for memory consolidation.

If you struggle to sleep when you are stressed because things keep going round and round in your head, try this great technique we use for helping us to fall asleep when the pressure is on.

 If you are looking to have a well-earned rest this is a great technique to use. If you are engrossed in this book right now, try it later if you are struggling to sleep!

- Close your eyes and begin counting backwards from 300.
- You may find your mind wandering back to the thoughts from the day. If this happens then force yourself to think of the last number you remember counting and count backwards again.
- We normally fall asleep before we have reached 200.

- We all process pressure and experience stress differently according to our personality.
- The MBTI is a good way to understand how you can best use pressure to energize you rather than stress you.

The best way to avoid stress is to understand how you prefer to handle pressure and then play to your preference.

V: Visualize success

Ordinary people believe only in the possible.
Extraordinary people visualize not what is possible
or probable, but rather what is impossible. And
by visualizing the impossible, they begin to see it
as possible.

Cherie Carter-Scott

Have you ever worked with someone who is really inspirational? Steve was one of those people. He had an extraordinary ability to take learning on board after a training course and really utilize it.

We had the pleasure of working with Steve and his peers for several days, exploring how they could create a peak-performing team. We were delighted to see that Steve was totally fired up as a result of the course. So much so, that he wanted to take his own team of 35 people through the course, so that they too could experience it.

Drawing on some of the course principles he had learned, such as 'shoot for the moon' and 'visualize success', Steve began to challenge himself. The course had been good, but could it be even better? What would make it even more impactful?

After a while, Steve came up with the idea of a successful celebrity walking in as a surprise during the course. They could talk to the team about success and could demonstrate how the theory of 'success' played out in practice.

Of course, it wouldn't be possible to hire a celebrity to speak – that would cost thousands of pounds which simply weren't available, on top of the usual costs of hiring the training facilities and so on. Nevertheless, fired up by how good he thought this idea was, Steve set about doing his research.

His efforts struck gold, quite literally. After only a short time searching, he found that a now-retired Olympic gold medal-winning athlete lived just down the road from where his offices were and that she had converted her old gym into a training centre, which could be hired out for a very reasonable charge. So at the very least, it would be possible to run the training from her house, which would be pretty unique.

He decided to ask the athlete if she would mind popping in at a break to say hello to his team. Much to his surprise, not only did she say yes, she said she would be delighted to come and do a talk for an hour and that the whole thing could be done within his budget.

It was a completely unforgettable day, exceeding even Steve's expectations – meeting the athlete, seeing her gold medal, and even spending time with the athlete's parents and her dog! Steve demonstrated that by simply visualizing the impossible, you could make it possible.

The athlete in this story was the 1992 Olympic 400 metre hurdles champion, Sally Gunnell. Sally wasn't one of those people who woke up at the age of six and suddenly realized that they had to win at the Olympics. Instead, she used to work in an office and therefore only trained part time. After winning the Olympic gold in 1992 she even thought about returning to work at the accountancy firm where she had been a researcher since 1986!

Sally was told in her youth that she was the 'wrong colour and wrong shape' to be an Olympic gold medal winning athlete. Didn't we warn you about the negative labels of others? So, Sally had to pull all the tricks out of the bag in order to succeed. One of the tools she used was the power of visualization.

Sally ran the Olympic final over and over in her mind, considering every possible scenario: getting off to a bad start, but recovering; leading all the way; running next to every competitor; being neck and neck with another competitor. Whichever visualization it was, the result was always the same – crossing the line first and winning gold. In fact, she described how she had used visualization so much (over 2,000 times) that when she actually ran the race, she didn't know whether she had really won it or only imagined it!

Read through these instructions and then close your eyes and try this exercise.

- Hold your arms out in front of you. Make sure that they are level.

- Imagine that your right arm has a bunch of helium balloons tied to it.
- Concentrate really hard on the image for about ten seconds and then open your eyes.

What has happened to your right arm?

Imagination versus reality

Many people find that when they attempt this visualization exercise, their arm mysteriously rises upwards. This is because the brain can't always differentiate between something that is real and something that is imagined very vividly. That's why you can wake up dripping in sweat with your heart pounding when you have a nightmare and why you might scream when you are watching a scary film even though there is no immediate danger to you.

It's not the visualization of the end goal that leads to performance improvement though, but visualizing the process of succeeding towards that end goal. Ainscoe and Hardy in 1987 found that gymnasts who visualized performing each individual twist and turn they would do – just like Sally Gunnell visualized running each step of the race – performed their routine with noticeably improved physical ability.

Imagination is everything. It is the preview of life's coming attractions.

Albert Einstein

Many top athletes know the power of visualization and use it to their advantage. Roger Bannister, the first man to run a mile in under four minutes, imagined himself at the start line and then visualized running the race over and over in his mind. When it came to the actual race, he astonished disbelievers who didn't think that a mile could be run in under four minutes.

Jonny Wilkinson, who kicked the winning points for England against Australia in the 2003 Rugby World Cup, visualizes by imagining his leg is a golf club and that he has to swing a shot just right with it, or that that there is a can of coke behind the goal posts that he has to hit spot on.

And perhaps most fascinatingly of all, when javelin thrower Steve Backley sprained his ankle and was left unable to walk, months before the 1996 Olympic Games, he feared he had no chance of competing. He had been on crutches for six weeks and was unable to train physically because of his injury. He was, however, still able to use the power of visualization to help him train mentally.

During his recovery, Steve imagined himself throwing javelins over and over again. By the end of this time in his 'mental gym' he had mentally thrown over 1,000 javelins. Astonishingly, he found that when he returned to competition, he achieved the same level of performance as he had done prior to the injury and was still on track to win a medal at the Olympics. He managed to win the silver, not bad for somebody who, weeks before, couldn't even stand properly.

While visualization is very popular within the sports world, its benefits extend to many areas. In 1988, psychologist Shelley Taylor found that students who practised mental rehearsal, while focusing on what they needed to do to get a high grade (like sitting at their desks going over lecture notes), improved their performance compared to those who just visualized receiving a high grade at the end of their exams.

The ability to visualize comes with practice, so take the opportunity now to develop this skill in relation to your goals.

- Find a quiet place where you will not be interrupted. Sit in a comfortable position and close your eyes.
- Focus on your breathing, breathe in deeply and let it go. Keep repeating this.
- Calm your mind. Say the word 'relax' to yourself in a soft tone.
- With a first person perspective, bring to your mind a movie of you at the time that you succeed in your goal.
- Who is there with you?
- How are they congratulating you?
- Are they shaking your hand or hugging you? If so, how does that touch feel? Strong, warm, gentle?
- Take a look around you, what else do you see?
- What sounds can you hear? Are they loud or soft?

- Allow the movie to play until it comes to an end.
- When it has finished, open your eyes slowly and recall the sensations you had in the visualization.

Because visualization is a skill, the more you can repeat it the more you can step into what you visualize. So when you are ready, perform this activity again and as you develop this ability, begin visualizing yourself performing the specific steps you need to take towards achieving the success you've seen yourself being rewarded for.

- Visualization allows you to mentally rehearse something going as you plan it.
- Visualization physiologically tunes you into what needs to be done, making it more likely you will succeed.
- Visualizing whatever it is you need to accomplish will make it seem more possible and therefore attainable.

 You will be able to improve the quality and quantity of your achievements by mental rehearsal, performing the steps you will need to take in order to accomplish them.

W: Winning ingredient

Modern society has put the cart before the horse. In the past we thought that if you worked hard and were successful, then you would be happy. Turns out we have gotten the order wrong all along.

Shawn Achor

We began the book by talking about the critical need to set goals that will make you happy. It has been our aim that you enjoy the experience of working towards your goal as well as reaping the benefits of achieving it – hopefully this is happening!

As we begin to reach the end of our journey, we want to revisit the notion of happiness and inspire you, because finding happiness may be even more important than you think. In fact, if you want just about any form of success, from finding and staying in a relationship, to living longer, to earning more, the research shows that happiness is a winning ingredient. Here's why …

In a fascinating study by Masters, Barden and Ford, two groups of 4-year-olds were asked to put blocks together as fast as they could. The groups were treated exactly the same apart from one key difference. Just before doing the task, the second group of children were asked to think about their happiest memory. In scientific terms, this means that they were 'primed to feel happy'.

The researchers then timed how long it took the children to complete the task and staggeringly, they concluded that their success rate and their speed in completing the task increased up to 50%.

And it turns out that it isn't only children who achieve more when they are happy. In a second study by Alice Isen in 1991, doctors were asked to make a medical diagnosis based on hearing a set of symptoms. This time, the participants in the study were divided into three groups – one group was just asked to make a diagnosis, a second group was asked to make a diagnosis, but given a medical journal to read beforehand to 'warm them up', and a third group was asked to make a diagnosis having been primed to be happy.

Just like the children, doctors who were primed to be happy showed an increase of up to 50% in the speed at which they were able to reach a medical diagnosis compared to both the other groups. They were also able to reach the correct diagnosis in half as many steps as the other groups.

So what was it that made the doctors so happy that their performance could increase so significantly? The answer: sweets. Yes, they were given sweets to make them happy. And they weren't even allowed to eat them until after the experiment, because it would change their blood sugar level.

Perhaps the next time you visit the doctor you should consider taking some chocolate with you!

Can you think of a time when you were in a good mood and really flew through a task, creating great results?

Conversely, can you think of a time when a bad mood got in the way of you performing at your best?

The benefits of being happy

Even more impressive is the result that happiness has on longer-term measures of success. It would seem that happiness can even predict how long you live for.

In a remarkable study, researchers had access to the novitiate essays produced by 180 nuns from the School Sisters of Notre Dame in 1932. These essays gave a small amount of autobiographical information about each nun, which they submitted as they took their final vows to enter the convent.

A group were asked to read the essays and rate how happy they believed the nuns were, based on the words that they wrote. The 180 nuns were then divided into quarters, with the 45 happiest nuns being classified in the top quarter and the 45 least happy nuns classified in the bottom quarter.

Astonishingly, it was found that by 1991 90% of the most cheerful quarter were still alive at the age of 85, versus only 34% of the least cheerful quarter. Similarly, 54% of the most cheerful quarter were alive at the age of 94 as opposed to only 11% of the least cheerful quarter.

What is particularly significant about this study is the uniformity of the lives that nuns lead. Much of the variability of factors that can impact on life expectancy, such as diet or access to medical care, were controlled for, making the results even more impressive.

The benefits of happiness on major life factors don't stop there. If you'd like to find more success in your career, you might be interested to find that Sonja Lyubomirsky, Professor of Psychology at the University of California, Riverside, has concluded through her research that happy employees:

- Are more productive
- Are less likely to experience job burnout
- Have less time off sick
- Are more likely to be successful as a leader
- Have higher levels of creativity
- Have higher levels of resilience
- Generate more sales.

Researcher Peter Totterdell even found that happy cricketers have higher batting averages!

And if that weren't enough, it would also seem that how much you earn correlates with how happy you are. Former Professor of Psychology at the University of Illinois, Ed Diener, studied how cheerful college students were when they entered college and how much money they earned when they were in their thirties. He found that students with greater cheerfulness in the first year of college earned more money nineteen years later. They were also less likely to experience long-term unemployment after college.

In a second study, this time carried out in Australia, young adults who described themselves as very happy at a particular time were more likely to have increased income during the following period. Similar results were obtained in a Russian study, even after having accounted for demographic variables.

In Chapter B (Begin with the end in mind) we argued that money doesn't necessarily bring happiness. Yet these results show that there *is* a link between success and money, but in the opposite direction to the one you might expect. So, it would seem that if you are interested in increasing your wealth, or your life expectancy or your career success, then you are well advised to focus on increasing your happiness.

Given the compelling causal link between happiness and success, the next logical question is, 'Can I increase my happiness?'

So if I'm not naturally happy, am I doomed to failure?

Although scientists believe that approximately 50% of your happiness level is genetically determined, this does leave plenty of room for improvement.

There are many exercises that you can do to increase your happiness, but we are going to share with you one of the simplest and most famous ways to increase it: express-ing gratitude.

Research by Dr Robert Emmons has shown that just the simple act of writing down five things that you are grateful for has the impact of raising your happiness over the next 24 hours. And if you do this every day for three weeks, it significantly increases your happiness levels for a stagger-ing six months.

How on earth does this work? Sometimes it just feels like we are surrounded by negativity, particularly through the media. For example, we remember hearing a story on the news about Oyster Cards being introduced across the London transport network. For anyone who doesn't know what an Oyster Card is, quite simply, they are a brilliant invention. You never have to buy a paper ticket ever again and the Oyster Card (which you touch in at the start and end of every journey) automatically works out the cheapest fare for you. Genius.

This was a good news story for London and millions of passengers. Yet the news bulletin focused on how bad it was that a few stations in London would now charge higher fares as a result of the Oyster Card. When you tune in to how the media report things, you become aware of just how negative they can be. They seem to put a black-cloud slant on virtually everything. Rather than finding something to celebrate in a news story, they find something to criticize instead.

When we listen to the media, it subconsciously trains our brains to look for what is bad in a situation. A Gratitude Journal, where we note down what we are grateful for, does the opposite, training you to look for what is good in a situation. And if you do it for three weeks, it begins to train your brain to automatically look for good around you, without having to consciously think about it each day.

The positive impact on your happiness levels of using a Gratitude Journal is a very robust psychological finding, so before you dismiss it as nonsense, have a go – you might really be surprised at the impact that this small act has upon your life.

 • Find a nice notebook. This will become your Gratitude Journal.
- Simply think about five things that you are grateful for. This can be anything, big or small, from the house that you live in to the taste of ketchup on your sausage sandwich.
- Write the five things down in the Gratitude Journal, with the date.
- Repeat this exercise for about three weeks, and longer if you choose.

You can also do this exercise verbally with your partner or children, over meals or at the end of the day and it is a great habit to get into.

- Our happiness levels can define our longevity, improve health, improve career success, and our ability to cope.
- By feeling positive you are likely to perform better at activities than if you are feeling negative.
- Become aware of outside forces that are trying to make you picture things negatively and distance yourself from them.
- Train your brain to appreciate regularly the things for which you are grateful.

 Achieving happiness can significantly help you to achieve success.

X: eXtra mile

Go the extra mile. It's never overcrowded.
Wayne Dyer

During their training, one question dominated the minds of Ben Hunt-Davis and the other seven British rowers going for gold in the coxed eights at the Sydney Olympics. That question was, 'Will it make the boat go faster?'

When they were faced with the choice of doing 45 minutes of training on the rowing machine or on an exercise bike ... *Will it make the boat go faster?*

On a Friday night, when they wanted to go for a beer after training ... *Will it make the boat go faster?*

And on 15 of September 2000, the team asked themselves whether they should attend the Opening Ceremony of the Olympic Games ... *Will it make the boat go faster?*

The answer was no, so they didn't. That's dedication. That's going the extra mile – and the athlete's village certainly wasn't going to be overcrowded with teams training that night!

Going the extra mile enabled Ben Hunt-Davis's 'underdog' team to win gold. Going the extra mile can enable you to win gold too. We love the question, 'Will it make the boat go faster?' Using this type of questioning is such a practical way of helping you to make decisions on a day-to-day basis that can make or break succeeding in your goal.

THINK ABOUT IT

What version of the question, 'Will it make the boat go faster?' do you need to ask yourself in order to achieve your goal?

In 2009, 24-year-old history graduate, David Rowe, might well have been asking himself the question, 'Will it help me get employed faster?' when he went through all of the options for getting a job. Like many other graduates, David was struggling to find work and had already received over 40 job rejections.

Inspired by hearing that during the Great Depression job hunters used sandwich boards to advertise, David decided to make himself stand out from the crowd by wearing a sandwich board down Fleet Street that read:

Job wanted. History Graduate, University of Kent. Interview me. Prepared to work first month FREE. Then hire me or fire me. Thanks for looking. David.

Although David admitted to feeling pretty embarrassed, his efforts paid off when he was quickly offered a job placement at a time when almost 1,000,000 16–24 year olds were out of work in the UK.

So it would seem that sometimes, being good isn't good enough. To succeed, you have to be prepared to go the extra mile.

TRY IT NOW! Stand next to a wall and make a small pencil mark as high as you possibly can (or just touch it if you don't want to make a mess!).

Now try again and make a mark even higher. Did you manage to go further?

When doing this exercise, most people give an extra push the second time and go even higher. This is the difference between good and great. But wouldn't it be powerful if you strove to get great results, first time, without having to be pushed? After all, you were initially told to reach as high as you possibly can – so go for it!

Work smarter

Going the extra mile doesn't even have to mean working harder. For example, David Rowe could have spent the same amount of time visiting recruitment agencies as he spent pounding the streets of London with his sandwich board. Ben Hunt-Davis could have spent the same 45 minutes on the exercise bike as he did on the rowing machine. But which of these two exercise options would have made the boat go faster?

It is the conscious thought, analysis or creativity that goes into identifying *what* is the difference, which truly *makes* the difference. Time and energy are both precious resources, and if you want to succeed, especially in the face of stiff competition, you have to invest these wisely and think proactively before others take advantage of that competitive edge.

This could be particularly differentiating if your competitors habitually spend their time and energy less optimally, taking the exercise bike or recruitment agency options, as in the examples above. You need to understand what can differentiate you positively from everyone else. Working this out requires you to understand the basis of your own behaviour, as you may well be falling into the trap of just acting habitually, holding yourself back.

Pick up a pen and sign your name.

How does it feel?

Next, pop the pen into the other hand and sign your name again.

How does it feel?

You will probably notice how strange it feels to sign your name with the opposite hand to normal. This is because you habitually do things in a certain way. Deviating from your habits feels strange.

How habitual behaviour works

When we learn something new, an area at the front of our brain, called the pre-frontal cortex, is involved. This is an energy-intensive part of the brain and it only has a limited capacity to process information. However, when something is done routinely, an area near the middle of the brain, called the basal ganglia, takes over instead. The basal ganglia run things on autopilot, freeing up our brain to think about other things and run the activity more efficiently. Hence a habitual behaviour is formed.

Here's an example. Remember when you first got into a car and learned to drive? There were so many things to think about; just working out which pedal did what required a lot of mental effort. And even when you finally passed your test and your excited friends piled in the back, you probably still had to ask them to shut up and let you concentrate when you approached a tricky junction. Several years down the line, you may well have had the horrifying experience of driving home on a very familiar journey, and suddenly realizing you had absolutely no recollection of the last ten minutes. Yet you safely navigated the car through all of those traffic lights. You were driving on autopilot.

As humans, we are predisposed to develop habits, and, more than that, once we are running on autopilot, there is a tendency to want to keep it that way. After all, changing the habit would require us to use some of that limited budget of working memory, so our brain makes us prefer autopilot.

THINK ABOUT IT

Imagine that you had to write with the wrong hand for the whole day. How would you feel at the end of the day?

Now, imagine that you had to write with the wrong hand for the next six months, say because you

189

had broken your dominant hand. How would you feel by the end of this time?

Most people say that they would feel exhausted and frustrated at the end of day one but by the end of six months, they would probably have got used to it.

Breaking habits does make your brain work hard but is possible with persistence and focus.

Consciously changing habits

People who achieve success in life are prepared to go the extra mile and put in the effort required to do things differently. At the heart of this is the ability to wake up from autopilot mode and constantly ask yourself if there is a better way of doing what you're doing.

This is one of the key reasons why repeatedly asking the question, 'Will it make the boat go faster?' was so critical. Asking this question made it a habit to look for opportunities to do things differently – a really powerful behaviour in itself.

The impact of going the extra mile

For years, owners of drugstores in those US states that are baking hot in the summer, such as South Dakota, had offered free iced water. It was nothing new (you could call it a habit!). But in the 1930s, Ted and Dorothy Hustead decided to metaphorically sign their names with the other hand.

Business had been tough for Ted and Dorothy, who owned Wall Drugstore located somewhere in the backend-of-beyond in South Dakota. With unfavourable conditions, tremendously hot sun coupled with eye-watering dust, most people simply drove past the store, eager to reach their destination as soon as possible.

Then, one day, Ted and Dorothy came up with the idea to advertise the fact they offered free iced water, and invite thirsty travellers into their store to cool off. They put signs along the highway, saying:

Get a soda … Get a root beer … Turn next corner … Just as near … To Highway 14 … Free Ice Water … Wall Drug.

The advertising was a masterstroke, with visitors encouraged to stop at what was known as the 'ice water store'. With the store gaining a reputation for its small town hospitality and untouched charm, the Husteads had to hire an additional five workers the following year to keep up with demand. The sign that had put Wall Drugstore on the map eventually started getting placed further and further away. Now, whether you're in Egypt, India or even the South Pole you can see a sign for the store.

Today, Wall Drug has developed into a 76,000-square-foot tourist attraction that is visited by thousands of visitors every day. What is fascinating is that they made the effort to do something different, to break habitual behaviour, and the results were quite remarkable.

THINK ABOUT IT

Think about what you want to achieve and ask yourself, whether there is anything that you are doing habitually that is holding you back from achieving your potential.

What would be a better habit to create?

USEFUL TIPS

- Switch away from bad habits that are holding you back
- Create new habits by bringing your attention to how each activity contributes to your success
- Time and energy are precious – use them smartly and don't accept, just because 'that's the way it's always been done,' it is the best way in your circumstances.

IF YOU REMEMBER ONE THING

Rather than exist with your current habits, create new beneficial habits that will help you to achieve.

Y: Yes!

Positive thinking will let you do everything better than negative thinking will.

Zig Ziglar

Once upon a time a shoe company sent one of its salesmen to a developing country to test the market for their products there. Within days, the salesman sent a message back to his boss saying, 'Nobody wears shoes here, I'm coming home.'

The shoe company decided to send another salesman; this one was considered to be more of an optimist. Within hours of arriving the salesman reported back to his boss, saying, 'Nobody wears shoes here, the market's ripe, send as many as you can.'

These two salespeople had a different perspective on what they saw. They were in the same place, saw the same thing, but had different opinions of what could happen. As with much in life, it's not always what happens, or what we're presented with, but our perspective in the situation that counts.

Optimism is about having hope or confidence in the future, and believing that our efforts will lead to a successful outcome. It's about saying, 'Yes this can and will be done', rather than simply saying, 'No, it can't be done.'

Why is optimism important for success?

Research into optimism has shown there are many benefits to having a more optimistic frame of mind. Hundreds of studies show that optimists do much better at school and university, on the playing field and at work. For example, Martin Seligman measured the optimism levels of sales people within an insurance company and found that the most optimistic people (the top 10%) sold 88% more than the least optimistic (bottom 10%).

If you consider winning a political election to be a measure of success, optimism seems to be a critical factor in achieving this. In the US in the past century, the candidate who was viewed as being more optimistic won 85% of presidential elections.

Optimists also have better health and have an improved ability to ward off infectious illnesses and even to avoid developing cancer. Research also indicates that they may even live longer. And, to top it all off, optimism is also related to marital satisfaction and good family relations.

So many of our areas described in our FLOURISH model in Chapter A are impacted directly by optimism. If you want more success in life, being optimistic is a real catalyst.

 Try to think of someone you know who is an Eeyore (a pessimist), someone who:

• Believes bad events will last for a long time

- Worries that a bad event in their life will have a knock on impact on other things
- Thinks that things that go wrong are their own fault.

Try to think of someone you know who is a Tigger (an optimist), someone who:

- Sees negative events as a temporary blip
- Doesn't let something going wrong in one area of their life affect other things
- Doesn't blame themselves when things go wrong.

The difference between optimists and pessimists

Martin Seligman spent over 25 years studying the difference between optimists and pessimists and his research reveals that there are three key things that differentiate optimists from pessimists.

1. Whether a person believes that the causes of bad events are **permanent** or **temporary**:
   - e.g. if you don't get offered a new job, is it because you aren't good at interviews (permanent – pessimistic) or because you didn't do well enough on the day (temporary – optimistic)?

2. Whether a person makes **universal** or **specific** explanations for negative events:

- e.g. if you break up from a relationship, was it because you aren't good at relationships (universal – pessimistic) or because you weren't dating the right person this time (specific – optimistic)?

3. Whether a person attributes events **internally** or **externally**:
   - e.g. if you get made redundant, was it because you weren't good enough at your job (internal – pessimistic) or because of a bad economic climate (external – optimistic)?

THINK ABOUT IT

Imagine that these three negative events had happened to you – you didn't get offered the new job, you broke up from a relationship or you got made redundant. Would you interpret these events optimistically or pessimistically?

Where do you lie on the Eeyore-Tigger continuum?

It is worth noting that you don't only have to be facing a bad event to demonstrate optimism or pessimism. An optimist will attribute good things:

- Permanently (things always go well for me) rather than temporarily (I just got lucky).
- Universally (I'm great at my job) rather than specifically (I did well at this task).

- Internally (I'm responsible for that good result) rather than externally (circumstances helped me).

One marshmallow or two?

In an intriguing 1970's study nicknamed the 'Stamford Marshmallow Experiment', Walter Mischel asked a number of 4-year-old children to wait alone in a room with a tempting marshmallow placed in front of them. The children were told that if they waited to eat the marshmallow until after the adult returned from an errand, they could have a second one.

Two types of responses split the children. The first type could not wait for the adult to return from the errand and they demolished the marshmallow. The second type displayed self-torturous distraction techniques for up to 20 minutes, until the adult returned – they were able to hold out. They were able to 'delay gratification' which means they were able to forgo something pleasurable in the short-term, in favour of receiving greater pleasure in the long-term.

What makes this study fascinating is that researchers revisited the participants again when they were teenagers. Strikingly they found that the children who were able to hold out for the marshmallow age 4, scored significantly better on the Scholastic Aptitude Test (SAT) when they were 18 years old. The marshmallow test was twice as good a predictor of SAT scores as IQ measures!

How is delayed gratification linked to optimism and success?

You may be able to identify with trying an exercise plan and then giving up after just a few weeks because you aren't seeing any visible results. You start to lose hope and confidence that you can lose weight. Slowly the temptation to stay in and watch television with a nice glass of wine overcomes your determination to go out for a run when it is cold and wet.

For quite a while we were suffering from this problem. However more recently, fortunately, we've had better results. We're delighted that we have finally found a genuinely enjoyable formula of diet and exercise that is working and we have managed to lose over 20 lbs each in just four months.

One of the key differences is that we now believe that we can actually lose weight, whereas for a long time it just felt impossible. We now know that it will be worth going out for an evening jog when it would be easier to stay home and tuck into a tasty take-away pizza.

Explaining this from a more scientific viewpoint, psychologists have concluded that optimism is linked to success because you have faith that forgoing short-term pleasures will be worth it in order to achieve long-term goals. In other words, optimism enables delayed gratification, which supports goal achievement.

How can I be more optimistic?

We've described the difference between optimists and pessimists and have outlined some of the benefits of being optimistic. So, the next important question is 'How can I be more optimistic?'

Remember the ABC model that you learned in Chapter F? This model can also be applied to help you to feel more optimistic, as the framework helps you to challenge negative and pessimistic beliefs.

For example:

Step 1. What was the Activating event? I got made redundant.

Step 2. What was the Consequence? I lost my self-confidence and now I'm worried about not being able to get a new job.

Step 3. What Belief underpinned that consequence? I'm not good enough at my job.

Step 4. Is there any other way to interpret this situation that Disputes your belief? Other people got made redundant and they were good so if you are laid-off, it doesn't mean that you weren't good enough.

Step 5. What is an Energizing alternative belief to adopt? It isn't my capability that was the problem, it was a poor economic environment. I'm good enough to get another job.

TRY IT NOW! Think of someone helpful, who you trust. You may wish to look back at your associations audit from Chapter R and refresh your memory of the people in your life who you identified as supportive and the kind of people you intend to share your goals with.

Ask this person to turn on their selective attention (see Chapter O for a reminder) and look for occasions when you are being optimistic and occasions when you are being pessimistic. Ask them to point these out to you.

If they spot you being pessimistic, get them to help you use the ABC model covered in this chapter and in Chapter F to come up with a more optimistic approach.

In Chapter X we covered the importance of going the extra mile, which might involve breaking some habits. This includes the way that you think – do you habitually interpret events optimistically or pessimistically? Given how many of the different areas in our life are impacted by our optimism levels, it is well worth putting effort into training yourself to think optimistically.

- Our view of events can tend towards being either optimistic or pessimistic; generally our goals are more attainable by seeing things optimistically
- There are many benefits to having a more optimistic viewpoint, including positive effects on our health, career and personal effectiveness
- Optimism can be learned by disputing negative thoughts and testing for alternative, more empowering scenarios. Try and make thinking optimistically a habit.

 Optimism is a powerful force that can help you to achieve your goals. One of the best things you can do to help yourself succeed is learn to increase your optimism levels.

Z: Zeal

Great energy or enthusiasm in pursuit of a cause
or an objective.
Definition of zeal, *Oxford English Dictionary*

In March 2008, a man and his fiancée had the great pleasure of travelling to Australia for the first time in their lives. They sat on the world-renowned Bondi Beach soaking in the moment, but also discussing something that they nicknamed, 'The Bondi Effect'.

They described the Bondi Effect as taking some conscious 'time-out', to step back from daily life, take a look at the bigger picture and work out what it is you want to get out of life. This is coincidentally exactly what our wise elders advised us all to do, as per the research in Chapter A. It was much easier for the couple to do this on Bondi Beach, away from it all, than in their normal day-to-day rat-race existence.

They eagerly went and bought a notebook and pen from an ocean-side shop and they began dreaming about what ultimate success would look like in their lives. No constraints, what would their perfect life be like? Alongside a dream of one day working together in an area that they loved, they set the goal of writing a book on a subject that they were passionate about.

So on the plane home from Australia, with many hours to kill, they sat and enthusiastically wrote the initial synopsis for their book. The first seed had been sown.

Soon after they landed back home, with their selective attention switched on, they quickly came across a talk that was happening at a local bookstore on how to get published. They went to the talk, keen to hear what the speaker had to say.

Much to their disappointment, the speaker spent the first thirty minutes telling the audience that what they wanted to do was virtually impossible, and everyone wondered why they had bothered coming. Although the rest of the talk was spent covering some very useful tips, not surprisingly, the couple left the bookstore feeling very despondent.

Despite the fact that their dream seemed like only a faint possibility, they didn't give up. However, they did have to balance their dreams with reality, as there were still many bills to pay. So they continued writing the book in their spare time. In any case, it was a pleasure, since it was a topic that they felt passionate about.

The next step was to begin generating some interest around their area of passion. So, on top of the experience they had already gained through teaching the subject, they learned how to set up a website. They also entered a national competition on their subject matter and trialled the specifics of the content through running workshops.

Eventually their energy paid off and they had the content of the book written out in full. So, as the speaker at the book talk had suggested all those months before, they started researching possible publishers to send their book proposal to, investigating what needed to go into a proposal and how to submit one.

Less than eighteen months after having sat on Bondi Beach, the by-now wife of the partnership felt ready to take what was to her a scary step – that of leaving her safe and comfortable full-time job. The couple felt that this was necessary to make enough time to realize their dream. Being self-employed was hard work and it was often frustratingly difficult to find the way forward. Yet they kept going. Once again, the focus was on earning enough money to pay the bills, given that they had given up the security of one full-time salary. Although the book was ready, the priority was financial survival.

They were on the brink of being ready to submit their book to a publisher for the first time. However, unbeknownst to them, the seeds of success had already been sown.

Here's the best part. One day in late 2010, completely and utterly out of the blue, an email landed in their inbox from a publishing consultant called Katie asking if they would like to write a book. The book was to be a new title in a series that had already sold millions of copies.

They didn't know how Katie found them – it was a case of having to pinch themselves to check if it was actually happening. In fact, she had followed the trail of successes they had made, including the website and videos of the competition. So, not only had they been offered a once in a lifetime opportunity to have a book published on the topic they were passionate about sharing, but what was being requested was effectively the content of a book that they had already written.

And you are reading it right now.

If you can dream it, you can do it. Always remember that
this whole thing was started with a dream and a mouse.
Walt Disney

Conclusion

We hope that the chapters of this book have inspired you to use our alphabet of success:

A – Get **activated** to step back from your life, work out what you want from it and take action to achieve it. Why wait for a wake-up call? Seize the moment now!

B – **Begin with the end in mind**, deliberately working towards what you want, rather than drifting through life until you reach a place where you are stuck.

C – Find lasting fulfilment in your life through striving to enjoy both the **current time and the future**. Always aim to enjoy the journey *and* the destination.

D – **Dare to dream.** Teach yourself to believe that you *can* do things that you really don't think that you can do.

E – Put in the **effort** needed to achieve your dreams, it's worth it, especially if you can enjoy that effort!

F – Overcome **fear** that holds you back.

G – Set specific and challenging **goals** to work towards, as they help you to achieve more.

H – Don't be afraid to aim **high**. Even if you don't quite make your goal, you'll achieve far more than if you just aim for average.

I – Break your seemingly impossible goals down into achievable **interim steps**, to help you to psychologically and practically progress.

J – **Just have a go**. Don't worry about failure, worry about the chances you miss if you don't even try.

K – **Keep going.** If things don't go well to start with, remember that it is worth the effort. Hold your head high and try again.

L – **Learn**. By taking action you have an opportunity to work out what works and what doesn't. You haven't failed by taking action – even if you don't reach what you were aiming for, you have succeeded in understanding more.

M – **Modelling** enables you to shortcut the amount of time and effort it takes to learn how to succeed, by copying the winning strategies and beliefs of others.

N – **Numbers** are useful things to keep track of when striving for your goal. As well as measuring your progress towards your goal, measure and monitor what effort you put in and how this impacts goal achievement.

O – There are **opportunities** all around you that will help you to reach your goal. Keeping your goal at the forefront of your mind helps your brain's power of selective attention to register those opportunities.

P – Before you can achieve your goal, there may be a lot of practical, logistical and mental **preparation** that you need to do. This preparation can be essential to long-term success and eventually you will see your hard work pay off.

Q – To keep yourself motivated, set yourself mini-targets, **quick wins**, which you can regularly achieve. This will ensure that you get a regular dose of the powerful chemical dopamine in your brain to keep you motivated.

R – The **Rosenthal Effect** demonstrates just how much impact the labels that other people put on us can have. Associate with people who support you and this will assist you to succeed.

S – Even if you have been told that you can't do something, remember that with some **self-belief** you can prove them wrong. Just because others say you can't doesn't mean they are right.

T – There are a whole host of people out there who can help you to succeed. Who would be a useful part of your winning **team**?

U – When striving to achieve, you may find yourself **under pressure**. Work out if pressure is your friend or foe and learn how to cope with it when it gets too much.

V – **Visualize success**. Picture your route to success and it can have very powerful results.

W – Remember that there is a very powerful **winning ingredient** when it comes to success and that is happiness. Focus on being happy and this will also help you to succeed.

X – What do you need to do to go the **eXtra-mile** towards achieving your goal? Always ask yourself, 'Will it make the boat go faster?'

Y – Strive to have a mind-set of '**yes**, I can do this', not 'no I can't' and you will be more likely to succeed.

Z – Live your life with **zeal**. Have great energy and enthusiasm for your goal and your hard work will pay off!

Good luck with your success!

> *I find that the harder I work,*
> *the more luck I seem to have.*
> Thomas Jefferson

Acknowledgements

With thanks to Jacqueline Hardt for reading, scrutinizing and enjoying our first draft of the book and to those who kindly gave their permission for us to cite their work.

Dedication

To our treasured family and friends who help us to enjoy the journey and reach the destination.

Index